BANKING AT THE GRASSROOTS

BANKING AT THE GRASSROOTS

Sekhar Chatterjee
Anil Bhuimali

ABHIJEET PUBLICATIONS
DELHI 110094

ABHIJEET PUBLICATIONS
2/46 Tukhmeerpur Extension
Delhi-110 094
Phone: 011-22960492, 65698474
E-mail: abhijeetpublication@gmail.com

BANKING AT THE GRASSROOTS

First Published 2011

ISBN 978-93-81136-47-8

PRINTED IN INDIA

Published by J.K. Singh for Abhijeet Publications, Delhi-110 094, Lasertypeset by Gaurav Graphics, New Delhi and Printed at Himanshu Printers, Delhi.

Preface and Acknowledgements

Agriculture can not develop unless credit facilities are made available to the farmers in the areas which are not viable. Supply of credit to such areas will be highly effective in rehabilitating the cultivators. Development of agriculture is only possible by injecting requisite doses of bank credit to the agricultural and allied activities. Hence the availability of banking and credit facilities is an essential condition for the economic development of the rural poor. To address the problems of credit in an effective way and to relieve the agriculturists from the clutches of moneylenders the Government has assigned the task mainly to the Regional Rural Banks. These banks have been playing a significant role in rural development.

The present study is intended to analyse the role of UBKGB, a regional rural bank, in agricultural development. It analyses the extent of credit requirements, credit disbursed and the prevailing credit gap. Apart from these, the problems related to utilization of loan, repayment performance and the impact of credit on borrowers' income, employment and standard of living are also dealt with in detail.

I am greatly indebted to Dr. Anil Bhuimali, my supervisor, and coauthor, who guided me from the start of the work to its completion. I express my sincere gratitude to him for his generous support with regard to reading my manuscripts and for his insightful, critical and extensive suggestions.

My indebtedness to all the faculty members of the Department of Economics, North Bengal University, is also invaluable for the help they extended in every aspect of the study.

I also thank my colleagues of P.D. Women's College and the principal of the same institution for their encouragement and help during the study. I here take the opportunity of expressing my deep gratitude to my respected father Late Ramapada Chatterjee, respected mother Late Nirupama Chatterjee and my elder sister Late Nanda Chakroborty for inspiring me to undertake higher studies.

I owe a lot to my wife Smt. Supriya Chatterjee for inspiring me throughout the period of preparation of the thesis by relieving me of the daily chores of domestic duty during the entire period of research.

Sekhar Chatterjee

Contents

1

The Problem

1.1 Introduction

Agriculture forms the core sector of the Indian economy as it accounts for nearly 21.7 percent of the aggregate national income and provides livelihood for more than 70 percent of the working population of the country.[1] A breakthrough in this sector is thus essential for placing the economy on a sound footing. The new technological possibilities thrown open by the recent researches in agricultural science have proved that the total yield per acre can be boosted up by applying the optimum package of farm inputs. This also indicates the desired adoption of new technology which demands higher and higher capital deployments. Shortage of finances has been identified as the major constraint in cases of marginal and small farmers to shift over to the new methods of cultivation. Creation of adequate credit facilities, therefore, has been identified as the principal solution for all Indian agricultural problems.

The multi credit requirements of agriculturists could not for obvious reasons be met by any single institutional agency. A multi-agency approach has, therefore been viewed as a better alternative. Recognising this the Government has assigned the responsibility of farm development to three agencies namely, co-operatives, commercial banks and regional rural banks. Each one of these is presumed to function as a part of a "System" having a close co-ordination with planning credit provision.[2] Further, they together are visualized as the instruments for rooting out the non-institutional agents from the scene over a period of time.

A comparative analysis of credit supply by different agencies over the periods suggests that non-institutional agencies continue to play a vital role in providing short-term credit to farmers. However, their share in relative terms has declined from 92.7 percent in 1951-52 to 36.8 percent in 1981 and to 25 percent by 1995-96. On the other hand, share of co-operatives, as percentage of the total agricultural credit has declined from 47.37 percent in 1995-96 to 34.20 percent in 2002-03 and then to 21.83 percent in 2005- 06. [3]

But an assessment of the macro level credit data reveals existence of huge credit gaps in the economy. This may be mainly because of the accumulated overdues with co-operatives and because of the imbalance between the demand and supply of credit channeled through the institutional agencies.

Considering the large and growing gap in meeting credit needs of developing agriculture and allied activities, the government encouraged commercial banks to provide more and more credit to agriculture and other allied sectors. The nationalization of 14 commercial banks in 1969 was regarded as a watershed in this direction.[4] These institutions have been financing agriculture till 1991 following government directives of rural development. But the Financial sector reforms recommended by Narsimham committee which seeks to minimise government control on financial institutions impose stringent accounting norms and give freedom to banks from mandatory rural lending of 40 percent to priority sector. This has resulted in a declining trend in the priority sector lending especially for agricultural loans by commercial banks. The growing demand for large amount of credit in agricultural sector for commercialization and diversification on one hand and the reduction in agricultural lending by the commercial banks on the other has put agriculture into a paradoxical situation. This has created an institutional emptiness at the grass-root level for the poorer section. If the rural areas are neglected, the really needy, small and marginal farmers will be left high and dry without any benefit from huge amounts flowing into the agricultural sector. In this context Regional Rural Banks (RRBs) as third arm have gained more importance in the rural credit system to cater especially to the weaker section of the society. The Uttarbanga Kshetriya Gramin Bank (UBKG) has been established in 1976 in the district of Jalpaiguri, West Bengal to meet the aforesaid objective.

1.2 The Problem

Agricultural credit is considered as one of the most important basis of inputs for conducting all agricultural development programmes. In India there is immense need for agricultural credit as majority of Indian farmers are very poor. Without adequate and timely credit they cannot make use of the essential agricultural inputs. Adequacy of credit is only one of the essential elements in a good credit system. Credit deficiency induces some of the borrowers to divert the loan amount for other purposes. Some borrowers are compelled to cut down their level of operation endangering viability of the project in question. It seriously affects their earnings and repaying capacity resulting in default and overdues. Hence availability of credit at the right time, at right doses and at a minimum cost is very important for smooth conduct of any economic activity. Undue delay in granting credit, frequent visits by the borrowers to bank and credit deficiency seriously affect the developmental activities. We can set the problems of our investigation in the following fashion:

- What is the relative performance of the UBKGB in meeting credit needs in time?

- To what extent credit has been granted by this bank?
- What is the experience of borrowers in securing credit from the bank and repaying it?
- Could the borrowers improve their economic condition?

These problems call for empirical studies. Initiation of a new study on the subject of agricultural credit will throw up additional information which will be of use in tackling problems relating to agricultural credit. This present study has been conducted to explore these problems.

1.3 Review of Literature

We can make a brief review of existing literature relevant for our purpose. Various yardsticks have been used to examine the impact of rural credit by RRBs by different scholars. These have also attempted to identify the factors responsible for improper utilisation of rural credit and analysed the reasons for default in repayment of loans.

Hanumantharayappa[5] (1977) studied the small farmers production credit requirement and repayment problems in the state of Karnataka and concluded that crop failure and diversion of income for other unproductive purposes were the main reasons for crop loan overdues.

Joshi[6] (1979) analysed repayment performance in agricultural loans and 14 common reasons for default of short and medium term credit were identified on the basis of response given by the defaulter borrowers. Among 14 reasons, some important reasons were low-yield returns, increase in domestic expenditure, new investment in land, gold, house, delay in payment by sugar factories and support of local political people.

Reddy and Reddy[7] (1979) observed that 80 percent of small farmers, 85 percent of medium farmers and 83 percent of big farmers repaid their credit timely.

Charan D. Wadhva[8] (1980) in his research work "An Analysis of the Working of RRBs in India" examined in detail the working of two selected RRBs – one in Haryana and the other in Rajasthan. The study revealed that RRBs inherited complicated procedural formalities from their sponsoring banks. The concluded that these banks were not able to meet the targeted disbursement of credit set by the Government of India.

A study conducted by RBI[9] (1980) on the viability of RRBs covered all aspects of the performances. The study concluded that RRBs had achieved the objective of helping the weaker section in rural areas by supply them credit to suit their requirements despite the constraint of limited areas of operation.

Chinappa Reddy[10] (1981) reported that most of the small farmers were non-willful defaulters, whereas most of the medium and large farmers were willful defaulters.

Pandey and Singh[11] (1981) reported that repayment of loan was the combination of ability to repay and willingness to repay the loan.

Balishter[12] (1983) found that the repayment capacity of small farmers was less as compared to medium and large farmers.

Mishra, Gupta and Sehgal[13] (1983) opined that the recovery percentage was more in small farms than in the Large farms.

Singh and Upadhyay[14] (1984) conducted a study on loan recovery of Regional Rural Banks in Bihar and found that the recoveries in RRBs declined continuously during the period 1978-80. The reason for declining or low loan recoveries were inadequate arrangement for recovery in bank branches and the shortage of funds with the borrowers to repay the loans either due to crop failure or on due expenditure on marriage ceremonies or other social functions or illness of family members. Inadequate follow up by banks for repayment and willful default were also important reasons for declining loan recoveries in RRBs.

The bankers suggest the measures for better recovery such as lending in cluster, timely reminders, tie-up arrangements with marketing agencies, support from government agencies and legal action against willful defaulters.

Vaishnaw[15] (1985) in his study (RRBs in India) examined the financial viability and performance of RRBs in rural lending in Rajasthan. The study showed that most of the RRBs could not meet the target of disbursement of credit set by Govt. of India and that they were still far away from the stage of financial viability. Yet they established their potential as a "Development Bank" of the rural poor. But the actual performance of RRBs was inadequate in terms of their geographical coverage and the level of their advances. The study showed that RRBs failed to take maximum benefits of refinance due to shortage of technical staff.

James[16] (1986) in his study showed that only 18 percent of the borrowers misused the credit granted by North Malabar Gramin Bank to various economic activities. The repayment performance of the loanees showed that majority of the defaulters belonged to the dairy scheme followed by self employment and business schemes.

Mishra[17] (1987) in his study found that expansion programme of commercial banks benefited the rural population considerably. RRBs had a major role in providing credit for rural development. Small and marginal farmers didn't benefit from such facilities. The study concluded that small and marginal farmers were unaware of banking facilities and were victims of money lenders.

Narasimbulu[18] (1988) studied the performance of RRBs in rural development Indian economy. The study revealed that RRBs were better than CBs and cooperative credit institutions. The study stated that all the PACS and rural branches of CBs should be brought under the floor of RRBs to have sound rural credit system in India.

Verma[19] (1988) analysed the impact of rural banking on the masses in Rajasthan. The study revealed that quantum of credit advanced per office increased year after year but the quantum of credit per office of nationalised banks, RRBs and CBs was lower than the average. Recovery of loans especially agricultural loans was inadequate in the state and the percentage of overdues on agricultural sector was as high as 58 percent.

Gangi Reddy[20] (1988) studied the role of RRBs in credit distribution with reference to Sree Anantha Grameena Bank in Anantapur district of Andhra Pradesh. The study revealed that the credit flow to the SC., ST. and backward caste (BC) category of population together is much lower than that the total credit flow to the upper caste people. This observation established the fact that in terms of credit disbursement even within the weaker section the upper caste people are more favoured than the people belonging to SC., ST., and BC categories.

Turan[21] (1989) in his study showed that due diversified lending, the PACS and RRBs in comparison with CBs were more accessible to the weaker sections of the rural masses. He found that the institutional agencies could not meet the credit needs of the borrowers to the extent of 24 percent. As regards the disbursement of credit, he opined that the RRBs were the most efficient banks followed by CBs and co-operatives. The study showed the delayed advances could perpetuate indebtedness among the borrowers.

Jain[22] (1989) in his work on 'Rural banks and Rural poor' examined the impact of RRBs on income and employment. The study revealed that loan assistance provided by RRBs to the downtrodden rural people created a positive impact on employment generation in rural areas. The net income per borrower was quite high in the post loan period as compared to the pre loan period.

Krishnan[23] (1990) in his study on "RRBs and Rural Development" observed that RRBs contributed greatly to the development of banking habits among the rural people through extensive branch banking and better customer service.

Bhatt[24] (1990) in his evaluation of IRDP found that 87.1 percent households had benefited from IRDP. About 86 percent of sample beneficiaries expressed the view that their family employment improved as a result of the rural development programmes.

D. Rajasekher and G.Suvarchala[25] (1991) in their study on "Institutional Credit and overdues" examined the problems of overdues. The study revealed that crop failure due to adverse weather condition and adequate income generation from the activities for which loan are sanctioned are important reasons contributing to the problem of overdues. The study further concluded that only a small proportion of defaulters cited the defective lending policies such as very high repayment schedules and high interest rate as the cause for overdues.

Naidu[26] (1991) examined the performance of CBs and RRBs in financing agriculture, industry under IRDP. The study observed that bank finance had a positive impact on income generation and employment opportunities through the overall impact on the beneficiaries was only marginal.

Shylendra[27] (1992) in his study on the performance of "Thungabhadra Gramin Bank" in Kranataka observed that the RRBs were facing the problems of low recovery of loans and mounting losses that led to most of them becoming non-viable. The study also revealed that loan disbursement had benefited mainly the better off sections of the beneficiaries.

Goswami[28] (1992) in his study showed that the advances of RRBs were diversified to different sectors and they brought about a significant change in the rural economy.

Betty Sebastain[29] (1992) studied the performances of RRBs in providing loan assistance to agriculture and non-agriculture sector and observed the major reasons for repayment of loans were failure of agricultural, illness of family members and rising consumption etc.

Reny Tyagi[30] (1993) analyzed the performance of RRBs of Ghaziabad District in Uttar Pradesh. The study observed that the main objective of the RRBs (Hindon Bank) has been fulfilled. The study also showed that both scheduled caste and scheduled tribes had been properly utilising credit facilities from the RRBs for production as well as consumption purposes.

Jaiprakash[31] (1994) studied that RRBs and PACs suffered from paucity of trained and honest personnel. The study also revealed that officials of CBs and RRBs indulged in corrupt practices while providing loans.

Sukhdev Singh[32] (1994) in his study "IRDP and District Development" examined the problems faced by the beneficiaries in getting loans at different levels and the time they had to spend for getting the loans. He found that some of the respondents paid more than 51 visits to various offices to receive the loan and the average time taken for getting a loan worked out to 7.4 months. Apart from paying several visits to the city and facing different hardships they also paid bribes at several offices to get the sanctioned loans. The further revealed that after availing loan only 5 percent of the respondents could improve their standard of living and about 33 percent of the respondents could experience some increase in their income levels.

A. Raja Rao[33] (1996) in his study on "Impact of the RRBs on income and Employment of Weaker Section" with special reference to NG Bank of Andhra Pradesh showed that in both Nalgonda and Narketpally branch areas, the beneficiaries belonging to the scheduled casts received the highest income from various schemes. He also found that in the Nalgonda branch, the small farmers got the highest incremental income and they got the lowest incremental income in Narketpally branch.

R.P. Singh and K. Sathees Babu[34] (1996) in their study on "Performance and prospects of RRBs" showed that the loan advanced by RRBs" have a direct and positive impact on the overdues in both per branch as well as per loan account cross the states in the country. Poor screening, lack of proper loan appraisal and possible diversion for non-productive purposes etc. were identified as the probable reasons for the poor business.

Veerashekharappa[35] (1997) in his research work "Institutional Finance for Rural Development" highlighted the adequacy of credit, cost of credit, misutilisation and impact of institutional finance in Hassan district of Karnataka. He found that the main reason for diversion of loan was the need for clearing the old debts of borrowers. The borrowers face many inconveniences in getting the loans due to the complicated loan procedures and the indifferent attitude of the bank. He concluded that bank finance had a visible beneficial impact on the farmer's well-being.

Lakshmi Narasaiah and Venkata Naidu[36] (1999) in their study investigated the working of RRB in financing IRDP. The study showed that the beneficiaries were aware of the IRDP. They however did not have detailed knowledge of various schemes under the programme. The study concluded that the beneficiaries had substantial increase in net income from the respective activities and a significant impact on employment and assets position.

Jayasheela and Bidar[37] (2000) examined the problems of overdues and the reasons for repayment of loans disbursed under different schemes from the RRBs in Karnataka. The study showed that about 65 percent of the beneficiaries did not repay loans. They also observed that borrowers did not get credit in time and this led to misuse of credit.

Benson Kunjukunju and S. Mohan[38] (2002) in their study on "Institutional Finance and Rural Development in Kerala" showed that nearly 32 percent of the borrowers engaged in the agriculture sector misused the loans obtained by them. The study observed that "inadequacy of credit" was the reason compelling them to divert the loan amount.

Pallavi Chavan, R. Ramkumar[39] (2002) in their study on "Micro-credit and Rural Poverty" found that in Bangladesh the practice of repayment from money lenders has resulted in the creation of "debt cycles".

Sharmistha Deb and Meenakshi Rajeev[40] (2007) conducted a field survey in the district of Hooghly, West Bengal and found that marginal farmers are increasingly relying on the trader class as a major source of credit for working capital. They also found that the repayment rates by these farmers are better than that of the comparatively better off farmers.

The above review of literature reveals that a good number of scholars have studied the repayment behaviour, problems of overdues and socio-economic impact of credit on income, employment and standard of living of the borrowers. Though a number of studies on Regional Rural Banks and rural credit are available, new studies are called for filling the information gaps. It is this need that has encouraged us to make a scientific study on the subject. The present study analyses the performance of UBKGB in meeting credit needs in time, cost of borrowing credit, time lag in getting credit, overdues and impact of credit on income, employment and standard of living of the borrowers.

1.4 Objectives of the Study

The following are set as the broad objectives of this study:

1. To assess the credit flow and its impact on income, employment and standard of living of the borrowers.
2. To analyse the problem of recoveries and overdues.
3. To ascertain the causes of overdues.
4. To investigate the time lag in getting credit from the bank.
5. To study the cost of credit incurred by the borrowers in getting loans.
6. To understand the policy implication of the credit use of farmers.

1.5 Hypotheses to be Tested

While making this study and keeping in view the objectives

to be achieved the following set of hypotheses have been formulated and the validity of which are tested in appropriate chapters :

1. The amount of credit given to the borrowers is not adequate to run the required activity.
2. There is delay in granting credit to the borrowers.
3. Majority of the borrowers have misutilised the credit.
4. There is an increasing trend of overdues.
5. Low return from the activity is the major reason for overdues.
6. There is no significant improvement in the income, employment and standard of living.

1.6 Scope of the Study

In this present study a holistic attempt has been made to analyse the role of the UBKGB in agricultural lending and to assess the flow credit in agricultural sector in the district of Jalpaiguri, West Bengal. Both quantitative and qualitative variables have been considered here for our study. The view of borrowers has been taken into consideration. Many works have so far been done by a good number of scholors on the issue of repayment bevaviour, problems of overdues and the impact of credit on the socio-economic condition of the borrowers. In this present study we would try to assess credit requirements of the borrowers, credit disbursed and the prevailing credit gap. It also gives an insight into the cost of credit incurred by the borrowers, time lag in getting credit, repayment performance and impact of bank credit on the borrowers in the district as no study has been initiated so far exclusively in the district. The study will suggest suitable solutions which if implemented, will bring about a sea-change in the agricultural sector. The present study would hopefully help the policy makers in policy formulations and implementation.

1.7 The Study Area and Methodology

This study unit of Uttarbanga Kshetriya Gramin Bank (UBKGB) in the district of Jalpaiguri, West Bengal, is based on the survey research technique. The bulk of information have been acquired from fields through observation and interview schedules. Personal interactions with the borrowers also gave insights into their problems. The multi-staged stratified random sampling design has been adopted for the present study. Borrowers were selected on the basis of multistage random sampling method. Three blocks namely Jalpaiguri sadar, Maynaguri block and Rajganj block were selected at random out of the total 13 blocks in the district. Two villages from each of the blocks were randomly selected. Thus we have six villages in the second stage. Again from six villages in the 3rd stage 160 borrowers comprising of marginal, small, medium farmers and agricultural labourers were selected randomly on the basis of maximum number of loanees.

Table1.1: Sample Size by Blocks, Villages and Borrowers

BLOCK	*VILLAGE*	*NO. OF BORROWER*
Maynaguri	Churabhander and Husludanga	53
Jalpaiguri	Choudhuri Para and Denguajhar	54
Rajganj	Kaluarbari and Mogha Para	53

1.7.1 Nature and Sources of Data

Based on the objectives and the hypotheses to be tested, the required data have been collected from both primary source and secondary source.

The secondary data have been collected from the Annual Reports through personal approach at the Head Office of the UBKGB, Coochbehar and also from NABARD for the period 1999-2006.

For evaluating the objectives of the study, Primary data relating to income, repayments, defaults and opinions of the borrowers have been collected with the help of Structured Schedule. The text of the schedule is given in Appendix 1.

1.7.2 Techniques for Data Analysis

Introduction of statistical techniques for analysis of data is necessary to draw meaningful conclusions. The objectively collected data has been suitably classified and arranged in tables in appropriate chapters. The following are the techniques adopted for analysis of data.

Co-efficient of Variation (C.V)

The co-efficient of variation is the most commonly used technique. With this it is possible to compare the variability of two or more than two series of their relative variation. It is called as Karl Pearson's Co-efficient of Variation. The Co-efficient of variation is calculated with the help of the following :

$$C.V. = \frac{s}{\overline{X}} \times 100 \qquad \text{Where}$$

$$s = \sqrt{\frac{\sum_{i=1}^{N}(X_i - \overline{X})^2}{N-1}}$$

$$\overline{X} = \frac{\sum X_i}{N}$$

Growth Rate

The growth rate analysis has been undertaken with a view to studying the changes in selected variables like deposits, advances relating to the UBKGB. The conventional growth model employed is based on the exponential function.

By assuming variable Y (deposits or advances) to be increasing approximately at a constant rate of 100 percent per unit of time 't' and further assuming that effect of disturbance is proportional to the trend value of Y_t, the following equation is adopted for estimating the compound growth rate:

$Y_t = ab^t v_t$ --------------- (1.1)

Where a = Y in the base year

V_t = error term

$b = (1 + g)$

By taking logarithm, the above equation is reduced to the following form:

$\text{Log } Y_t = \text{Log } a + t(\text{Log } b) + \text{Log } V_t$ -------- (1.2)

Where Log a and Log b are the Parameters of the function obtained by OLS method.

Defining

$Q_t = \text{Log } Y_t$

$X_t = t$

$A = \text{Log } a$

$B = \text{Log } b$

$U_t = \text{Log } V_t$

Equation (2) can be written as

$Q_t = A + X_t B + U_t$ ----------------- (1.3)

With the help of above equation, the value of g is obtained as

$\text{Log } b = B$

$B = \text{Antilog } b$

$B = 1 + g$

$g = B - 1$

For effective comparison, the growth rate arrived at with the help of equation (3) is multiplied by 100 to obtain percentage change in the variable concerned.

Regression Analysis

It is the basic technique for measuring or estimating the relationship among variables.

In order to examine the impact of bank deposit and total cropped area on agricultural advances, the log-linear multiple regression function has been used.

The regression co-efficient of $X_1, X_2, X_3, \ldots, Xn$ are determined by solving simultaneously the normal equations. The formula of multiple regression analysis is written as

$Y = a + b_1x1 + b_2x_2 + \ldots\ldots + b_nx_n$

Where Y = Dependent variable (agricultural advances)

$b_1, b_2, \ldots\ldots, bn$ = Regression Co-efficients

$x_1, x_2, \ldots\ldots, xn$ = Independent Variables

a = Intercept.

Rank Correlation Co-efficient

When the data are of a qualitative nature this method is used. In our study this method has been used to examine the similarity in the rankings of problems faced by different farm categories in six selected villages. The rank correlation co-efficient is given by the formula

$$R = 1 - \frac{6\sum di2}{n^3 - n}$$

Where di = difference of ranks.

n = number of problems.

Chain Base Index Numbers

In the chain base method the comparisons are made with the immediate past (preceding year) and accordingly the data (for the two periods being compared) are relatively homogeneous.

Chain base indices (C.B.I.) are obtained on multiplying the link relatives (L.R.) successively. Thus

$$\text{C.B.I for any year} = \frac{\text{current year L.R. ? preceding year C.B.I.}}{100}$$

Test :

Chi-square test

Chi-square (X2) test has been used to test the goodness of fit. When the observations are classified according to two attributes and the observed frequencies Oi in the different categories are shown in a contingency table. We want to test on the basis of the cell frequencies whether the two attributes are independent or not. In our study the test statistic is

$\chi^2 = \Sigma(O_i - E_i)^2/E_i$

Where O_i = observed frequencies.

E_i = expected frequencies.

T-test

The test statistic t is used in our study to know the significance. The test statistic used is

$$t = \frac{\overline{X} - \overline{Y}}{S^2\sqrt{\frac{1}{n1} + \frac{1}{n2}}} = t_{n1} + n2 - 2$$

$$S^2 = \frac{n_1 S_1^2 + n_2 S_2^2}{n_1 + n_2 - 2}$$

Where X and Y are means of two Samples.

n_1 and n_2 are the sizes of two Samples.

S_1 and S_2 are standard deviations of the two samples. the computed value of t has been compared with tabulated value of t for $n_1+n_2 - 2$ degree of freedom at 0.05 level of confidence.

Analysis of Variance (ANOVA)

Analysis of variance test has been applied in order to test for differences among more than two groups of data, where more than two means involved in the analysis. One-way analysis of variance test has been used in our study.

Post Hoc Test

It is Bonferroni method of multiple comparison. Whenever ANOVA results turn out to be statistically significant, the data have been subjected to further analysis to identify the pair(s) of means that are significant.

1.8 Socio-Economic Profile of the Study Area

Profile of the Study Area

The progress of agricultural sector of any region primarily depends upon the agro-economic climatic conditions of the region. In other words, the agro-economic climatic conditions serve as the basis of the development and well-being of farmers which in turn widen the scope of more capital investment in agriculture. This results in better production, better income and better repayment. It is, therefore necessary to have a discussion on the agro-economic-climatic factors.

Population

The total population of the district as per 2001 census is 34 lakh comprising of 17.5 lakh males and 16.5 lakh females. Of the total population 37 percent are SC and 21 percent are ST. The major ethnic groups in the district are Toyas, Rajbanshi, Ravas, Garos, Mech, Santhals, Madeshia and Oraon. The literacy rates among the male in the rural & urban areas are 70.75 percent and 86.27 percent respectively. While the literacy rates among the women in the rural & urban areas are 47.97 percent and 80.73 percent.

Climate

The district has a moderate tropical climate with quite heavy rainfall during monsoon. The cold season is from mid November to the end of February. This is followed by the hot season from March to May. The Period from June to about the beginning of October is the south-west monsoon season. October to mid November constitutes the post-monsoon season. The minimum temperature is at 10.7 oc and the maximum temperature is at 23.6oc.

1.9 Agro-climatic Features

Rainfall

The Jalpaiguri district has a moderate tropical climate with heavy rainfall during the monsoon. Rain is received in the district in varying intensities almost in every month barring December and January, although the district has a normal rainfall of 3119 mm.

Land Utilization Pattern

The land utilisation pattern of the district is presented in table 1.2. The net sown area of Jalpaiguri district came is 228000 ha. The area under forests is 174565 ha. The fallow land accounted for cultivation is 3250 ha for Jalpaiguri district.

Table 1.2: Land Utilization Pattern in the Study Area

SL. NO.	*PARTICULARS*	*JALPAIGURI DISTRICT (IN HA)*
1.	Area under forests	174565
2.	Net sown area (ha)	228000
3.	Land not available for cultivation	3250
4.	Fallow land	4190
5.	Geographical area	622700

Source: District Statistical Hand Book, Jalpaiguri, 2001.

Irrigation

In the district the net irrigated area is 84220 hectares. Out of this 57710 hectares are canal irrigated, 5670 hectares are irrigated by wells and 20840 hectares are irrigated by other sources.

River System

The rivers which are numerous and flow north-south, originate from Sikkim, Bhutan and Darjeeling hills and can be divided into two systems, namely, the Brahmaputra system and the Ganga river system. The Brahmaputra river system contains Tista, Jaldhaka, Torsa, Kaljani, Raidak and Sankosh while the Ganga river system contains the Mahananda with its tributaries.

Soil

The soil in the district is more or less porous throughout and, therefore, waterlogged are almost absent. Only on the southern parts there are a few marshy places which do not dry up completely in the summer. The greater part of the district is covered with alluvium ranging from pure sand to clay. In most parts of the district the soil is a sandy l0am, but in the basin between the Tista and Jaldhaka rivers it is hard, black and clay.

Major Crops

The district is predominantly agriculture oriented. The major crops of the area are paddy, jute, tobacco, potato and tea. Rice is the principal crop in the district. Pulses like musur, mug, gram and oilseeds are also grown.

1.10 Limitation of the Study

Time and money being the main constraints, the study has been confined to only a few villages of the district with a total sample of only 160 respondents. However, proper care and considerate thought have been exercised in making the study as systematic as possible.

1.11 Definition of the Concepts Used

Small Farmer (SF)

The cultivators whose holdings are between 2.5 to 5 acres.

Marginal Farmer (MF)

The farmers whose holdings are less than 2.5 acres.

Medium Farmer (MF)*

The farmers whose holding are in between 5 to 10 acres.

Agricultural Labourers (AL)

Those who do not possess cultivable land but who derive income from work in agricultural operations by way of wages.

STUDY AREA

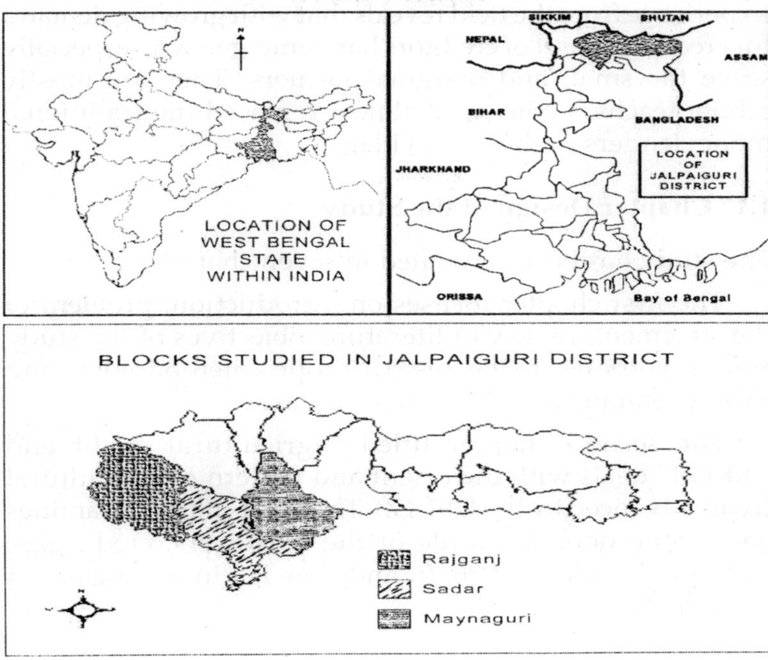

Outstanding Loans

The amount left with the borrowers for realization on a particular date are called outstanding loans. Outstanding loans are estimated total borrowings minus amount repaid.

Amount Overdue

A part of the outstanding loans becomes overdue loan if not realized within certain definite time limit. It is defined as : overdues are equal to the amount due for payment minus amounts actually repaid.

Moneylender

A moneylender is a person receiving major part of his income from money lending.

Baniyas

Experience from the field reveals that with growing demand for credit a new set of creditors have emerged who especially serve the small and marginal farmers. They are mostly school teachers who have almost replaced the traditional moneylenders in the rural villages.

1.12 Chapter Design of the Study

The study has been presented in seven chapters.

The first chapter focuses on introduction, problem of the statement, review of literature, objectives of the study and hypotheses to be tested, scope, methodology and socio-economic profile of the study area.

The second chapter titled "agricultural credit and UBKGB" deals with the extent and pattern of agricultural credit advanced by the UBKGB. The third chapter examines the socio-economic profile of the borrowers, credit gap, cost of borrowings of credit and time lag in getting credit from the bank.

The fourth chapter deals with experience of the farmers with the bank loans.

The fifth chapter evaluates the utilisation of credit, repaying capacity, repayment performance of the borrowers and reasons for overdues.

The six chapter 'Impact of Agricultural Credit' is an attempt at assessing the impact of the loans on the sample borrowers especially on the variables employment, income and standard of living. The last chapter viz., chapter seven, presents conclusion and suggestions.

NOTES AND REFERENCES

1. See the data from the *Economic Survey 2006-07*, p.s. 5.
2. V. G. Paramjit Malya (1980), *Agricultural Finance by Commercial Banks*, Ashish Publishing House, New Delhi.
3. See the data from
(a) *Economic Survey*, 1998-99.
(b) All India Debt and Investment Survey, 1981, *Sarvekshana*, July 1986.
4. S. B. Hosamani, *Performance of Regional Rural Banks- A Study*, Anmol Publications Pvt. Ltd., New Delhi, 2000.
5. G. W. Hanumantharappa, *Small Farmers Production Credit Requirement and Repayment Problems, A Study in Doddabalarpur Taluk, Bangalore District*, University Agriculture Science, Bagalore, 1977.
6. M. K. Joshi, Agricultural Loans, An Appraisal of Repayment Performance, *Financing Agriculture*, 11(1), pp. 13.2.1979.
7. T.S. Reddy and C. R. M. Reddy, "Recovery of Loans- A Study of Proddatur Co-operative Agricultural Development Bank," *Indian Co-operative Review*, 16(4), pp. 334-41, 1979.
8. Charan D. Wadhva, *Rural Banks for Rural Development*, Macmillan Company India Ltd., New Delhi, 1980.
9. "Viability of RRBs"-A Study, *RBI Monthly Bulletin*, XXXV, March 1981
10. Chinappa Reddy, "Analysis of Overdues Among Farmers in Srinivaspur taluk of Kolar District", M.Sc. (Agriculture) Thesis,

Unpublished, University of Agriculture Science, Bangalore, 1981.

11. Pandey, and Singh, "Risk and Credit Management in Changing Agriculture", *Indian Co-operative Review,* 9(1), pp. 91-103, 1981.

12. Balishter, "Evaluation of Repayment Capacity of Farmers", *Indian Co-operative Review,* 21(1), pp. 90-93, 1981.

13. Mishra, Gupta and Sehgal, "Working of Farmers Service Soceity in Jabalpur District (M.P.) with Reference to Farm Loans", Indan Co-operative Review, 21(2), pp. 200-212, 1993.

14. Singh and Upadhyaya, "A Study of Loan Recovery of Regional Rural Bank in Bihar", *Financing Agriculture,* 16(2), pp. 37-39, 1994.

15. Vaishnaw, *RRBs in India,* Rawat Publications, Jaipur, 1985.

16. James, Regional Rural Banks and Rural Development, A Case Study With Reference to North Malabar Gramin Bank, Cochin University, Cochin, M. Phil., 1986.

17. M. N. Mishra, *Appraisal of Credit Facilities Provided by Banking Institutions in Rural Development,* Pragathi Prakashan, Meerut, 1987.

18. Narasimbula, *RRBs in Rural Development,* Sri Venkiteswra University, Tirupati, Ph. D. 1988

19. Verma, *Rural Banking in India,* Rawat Publications, Jaipur, 1988.

20. Gangi Reddy, "The Role of Regional Rural Banks in Credit Distribution', *Kurukshetra,* May, 1998.

21. M.S.Turan, *Institutional Finance in Rural Development,* Herman Publishing House, New Delhi, 1989.

22. M. K. Jain, *Rural Banks and Rural Poor,* Printwell Publishers, Jaipur, 1989.

23. C. Krishnan, "Regional Rural Banks and Rural Development", *Yojana,* Vol. 33, No. 24, January 1-15, 1990.

24. G. D. Bhatt, *Rural Development Programmes in India- An Evaluation of IRDP,* Shanti Publications, New Delhi, 1990.

25. D. Rajasekhar and G. Survarchala, "Institutional Credit and Overdues", *Economic and Political Weekly,* July 27, 1991.

26. M.C. Naidu, *Financing of IRDP in India,* Discovery Publishing House, New Delhi, 1991.

27. M. S. Shylendra, The Impact of Institutional Credit on Rural Poor With Special Referance to the Performance of RRBs in Karnataka, Bangalore University, Bangalore, Ph. D., 1992.

28. S.N. Goswami, "RRBs- Land Mark in Rural Banking", *Kurukshetra,* Vol. XL, No. 10, July 1992.

29. C. Sebastian, Betty, Regional Rural Banks and Rural Development, A Case Study With Special Reference to South Malabar Gramin Bank, University of Kerala, Thiruvananthapuram, M. Phil., 1992.

30. Reny Tyagi, *Role of Banks for Rural Development in India,* Sarup and Sons, New Delhi, 1993.

31. Dr. Jaiprakash, Role of Institutional Rural Credit Development in Etawah District in U. P., Project Report, ICSSR, New Delhi, 1994.

32. Sukhdev Singh, *IRDP and District Development,* Deep and Deep Publications, New Delhi, 1994.

33. A. Raja Rao, "Impact of the RRBs on Income and Employment of Weaker Sections", *Kurukshetra,* Vol. XLIV, No. 10, July, 1996.

34. R. P. Singh and K. Sathees Babu, "Performance and Prospects of Regional Rural Banks-An Appraisal", *Kurukshetra,* July 1996.

35. Veerashekharappa, *Institutional Finance for Rural Development,* Rawat Publications, Jaipur, 1997.

36. M. Lakshmi Narasaiah and Dr. G. Venkata Naidu, *Role of Banking in Rural Development,* Discovery Publishing House, New Delhi, 1999.

37. Dr. Jayasheela and R. R. Birdar, "Rural Finance, A Village Study", *Kurukshetra,* Vol. 48, No. 6, New Delhi, March 2000.

38. Dr. Benson Kunjukunju and Dr. S. Mohanan, *Institutional Finance and Rural Development,* New Century Publications, New India, 2002.

39. Pallavi Chavan and R. Ramakumar, "Micro-Credit and Rural Poverty-An Analysis of Empirical evidence", *Economic and Political Weekly,* March 9, 2002.

40. Sharmistha Deb and Meenakshi Rajeev, "Banking on 'Baniyas' for Credit", *Economic and Political Weekly,* January 27, 2007.

2

Agriculatural Credit and UBKGB

2.1 Introduction

Agriculture is the backbone of nation's economy and the improvement in agricultural productivity is of paramount importance today. It not only provides food and other wage goods to our population, but also ensures a strong base for the development of the industrial sector. Agriculture, like industry needs short, medium and long term investible funds. For the development of agriculture, farmers need credit for the purchase of material inputs such as seeds, fertilizers, pesticides and so on. Without adequate and timely credit farmers can not make use of these essential inputs. The use of better quality of inputs would mean greater demand for rural credit. If we are all concerned about increasing total agricultural output in the short period, we must provide credit first and foremost. "Availability of credit to agriculturists at economic rates interest, for agricultural purposes and at the time credit is needed by them, is an essential condition for the healthy and sound functioning of an agricultural economy."[1] One fact is unbeatable, adequate credit is sine-qua-non for agriculture. Hence availability of banking and credit facilities is an essential condition for the economic emancipation of the rural masses.

The rationale of setting up of RRBs, as a third constituent of the rural credit system, is to meet the growing demand for credit for modernization and commercialization of agriculture. The UBKGB that came into being during 1976 in Jalpaiguri district of West Bengal is based on the same line of thinking. The total agricultural credit from the UBKGB has steadily increased from Rs. 207.00 lakhs in 2002-03 to Rs. 761.75 lakhs in 2004-05. At the state level the share of agricultural credit by the RRBs is insignificant and at the national level, the share of RRBs is also insignificant between 8 per cent to 10 per cent during the same period.

2.2 Purposes of Credit

In view of the financial requirements of the rural borrowers. the RRBs provides loans for three purposes :-

1) Short -Term Credit

Short term credits are required for raising crops. These loans are disbursed either atRabi or Khariff season in each year. These loans are made available on the basis of the land under cultivation or to be cultivated. The scale of finance depends on the basis of the cost of cultivation per acre of each crop.

2) Medium -Term Credit

Medium-term loans may be necessary for purchasing livestock, farm machinery, making arrangement for irrigation, or making temporary improvement over land etc. The repayment period varies from 15 months to 5 years.

3) The Long-Term Loans

The farmers need long-term credit for the purchase of land, costly machineries like tractors, power tiller, for effecting permanent improvements on land like sinking of wells, for installation of tube well etc. These loans are for long-periods of more than 5 years.

In the present study we have combined medium term and long term loans together under "term loans."[2]

2.3 Trend in Flow of Ground Level Credit

Since the RRBs have been allowed to work on the same lines on which the scheduled CBs have been working, their head of advances are almost the same. In other words, the RRBs like any other scheduled CBs allow advances to their customers in the form of crop loans, term loans, loans on non-farm sector and other priority sector etc. Therefore, the UBKGB is extending credit under all these heads. The total advances given by the UBKGB are shown with the help of Table 2.1.

Table 2.1 : Total Advances by the UBKGB

Year	*Total Disbursement (Rs. in lakh)*	*Chain Base Index No.*
1999	232.06	100
2000	297.30	128.11
2001	283.87	95.48
2002	556.73	196.12
2003	562.09	100.96
2004	1040.25	184.86
2005	1798.19	172.86
2006	2064.18	114.79

Source: District Credit Plan, 1999 - 2006.

The ever increasing trend of advances disbursed by the UBKGB in the district is shown with the help of figure 2.1. Table 2.2 and the figure 2.1 under study make it clear that there is a continuous increase in advances extended by this bank in the district. Through there has been a constant increase in these advances, the rate of increase has been declining every year since 2004, as it has come down to 72.86 percent in 2005 over 2004, to 14.79 percent in 2006 over 2005 as against 84.86 percent in 2004.

Similarly the advances per branch have also increased from Rs. 5.95 lakh in 1999 to Rs. 14.05 lakh in 2003 to Rs. 51.61 lakh in 2006 by registering a 8.67 fold increase during the period 1999-06 (Table 2.2).

Table 2.2 : Advances Per Branch of the UBKGB

Year	*Advances Per Branch (Rs. in lakh)*	*Fixed Base Index No.*
1999	5.95	100
2000	7.43	124.87
2001	7.10	119.32
2002	13.92	233.93
2003	14.05	236.12
2004	26.01	437.12
2005	44.96	755.59
2006	51.61	867.35

Source: Date Supplied by the UBKGB Branches.

The index numbers based on 1999 have also become 233.93 in 2002 and 867.35 in 2006. Thus the UBKGB has achieved a commendable success in credit distribution since 2002 which is also proved by the respective fixed base index numbers.

2.4 Growth of Agricultural Credit

The UBKGB as a RRB does not lay more emphasis upon the commercial activities but makes all possible effects to meet the credit requirements of agriculturists and other weaker sections of the society especially in the rural areas. The UBKGB is extending credit under two heads viz, agricultural and non-agricultural sectors of the economy.

The extent and pattern of agricultural credit given by the UBKGB is given in table 2.3. The agricultural credit in the district has increased at a considerably high rate in recent years. From the level of Rs. 60.96 lakhs in 1998-99, it has increased to the level of Rs. 805.57 lakhs in 2006. It has increased by 13.2 times between 1998-99 and 2005-06 registering a compound growth rate of about 24.11 percent.

Table 2.3 : Year-Wise Position of Agricultural Advances by the UBKGB

Year	*Total advances (Rs. In lakh)*	*Percentage*	*% change over previous year*
2000	61.12	20.56	0.26
2001	54.00	19.02	-11.65
2002	290.88	52.25	438.67
2003	207.00	36.83	-28.84
2004	390.84	37.57	88.81
2005	761.74	42.36	94.89
2006	805.57	39.03	5.57

Source: NABARD, Kolkata, 2000 – 2006.

The share of agricultural credit to total bank credit does not show any particular phenomenon, but a decline trend is noticed since 2002. This percentage which was 20.56 percent in 2000 has increased to 39.03 percent in 2006, accounting for 18.47 percent increase over the base year. When the percentatge change in credit is worked out it is seen that except 2001 and 2003 in all the years the credits are found to be increasing, but its magnitude is much less during the period from 2003 to 2006 in comparison to the year 2002.

Not only the amount of agricultural credit has increased, the number of borrowers has also increased rapidly from about 1145 thousand in 1999 to about 1952 thousand in 2006. Since the growth of amount of loans advanced is much more than the growth of number of borrowers, the amount of loans per borrower has increased from Rs. 5324 in 1999 to Rs. 41269 in 2006. Increase in the amount of credit per account indicates a vertical expansion of credit. It means that the need to provide more credit to the farmers is considering by the UBKGB. The diagrammatic representation of the trend of agricultural credit is shown in Figure 2.2.

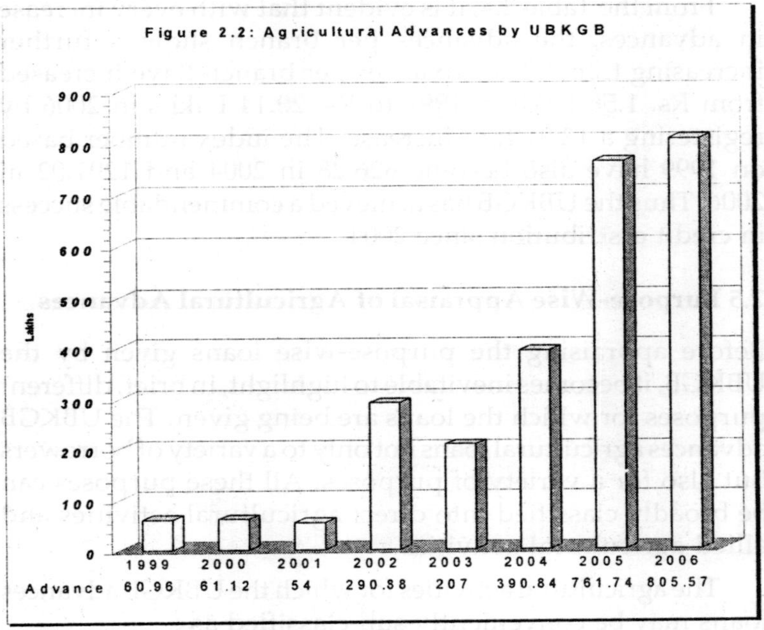

2.4.1 Per Branch Agricultural Credit

In order to show the trend of agricultural credit by the UBKGB, we have also calculated the advances per branch of the bank under study. The same are give in Table 2.4.

Table 2.4: Agricultural Advances Per Branch

Year	*Total Advances*	*Advances Per Branch (Rs in Lakh)*	*Fixed Base Index Number*
1999	60.96	1.56	100
2000	61.12	1.53	98.08
2001	54	1.35	86.54
2002	290.88	7.27	466.03
2003	207	5.18	332.05
2004	390.84	9.77	626.28
2005	761.74	19.04	1220.50
2006	805.57	20.14	1291.02

Source: District Credit Plans, 1999-2006.

From the Table 2.4, it is evident that with every increase in advances, the advances per branch show a further increasing trend. The advances per branch have increased from Rs. 1.56 Lakh in 1999 to Rs. 20.14 Lakhs in 2006 by registering a 12.91 fold increase. The index number based on 1999 have also become 626.28 in 2004 and 1291.02 in 2006. Thus the UBKGB has achieved a commendable success in credit distribution since 2004.

2.5 Purpose-Wise Appraisal of Agricultural Advances

Before appraising the purpose-wise loans given by the UBKGB, it becomes inevitable to highlight, in brief, different purposes for which the loans are being given. The UBKGB advances agricultural loans not only to a variety of borrowers but also for a variety of purposes. All these purposes can be broadly classified into direct agricultural activities and allied agricultural activities.

The agricultural activities for which the UBKGB advances loans may be conveniently sub-classified as :

(A) Direct agricultural activities; and

(B) Allied agricultural activities.

2.5.1 Direct Agricultural Activities

The direct agricultural activities include the following purposes for which a rural borrower can get loans from the UBKGB:

(1) to finance crops or crop loan schemes;

(2) to finance drought animals i.e. bullocks and he-buffaloes;

(3) to finance tube wells/pump sets and other tractor implements;

(4) to finance land development projects;

(5) to finance agricultural implements; and

(6) to finance storage/market yard.

2.5.2 Allied Agricultural Activities

The allied agricultural activities include advances given by the UBKGB to finance dairy farming, poultry farming, goat units, sheep units, piggery units, fisheries, gobar gas plant, etc.

The purpose-wise agricultural advances by the bank is shown in Table 2.5. From the credit share of the UBKGB under direct agricultural activities and allied activities we find that for the year 2002-.03, out of total plan outlay of Rs. 361 lakhs of the district, the target of the UBKGB under direct agricultural activitics was Rs. 190 lakhs representing 52.63 percent while the overall achievement of the bank was 92.03 percent compared to 67.85 percent under allied activities. The overall credit share under direct agricultural activities in terms of achievement was 60.11 percent.

During the period 2005-06, the share of the bank under direct agricultural activities has increased both in terms of the target (82.24 percent) as well as the achievement (86.60 percent). While the credit share under allied actives has decreased both in term of target (17.73 percent) as well as the achievement (13.40 percent) during the same period.

Over the period from 2002-03 to 2005-06, the target share of credit of the bank under direct agricultural activities is 80.48 percent and achievement is 83.62 percent. While the credit share under allied activities has rapidly decreased both in terms of target (19.52 percent) as well as achievement (16.38 percent) over the whole period. The overall achievement under direct agricultural activities is more than that of allied activities over the period from 2002-06. The increasing trend of direct advances is shown is figure 2.3.

From the above discussion it is clear that the share of the bank under direct agricultural activities both in terms of target and achievement has increased over the year in the district. This indicates the extent of the success of bank's policy of extending direct assistance to agriculture.

Figure 2.3 : Direct Agricultural Advances by the UBKGB

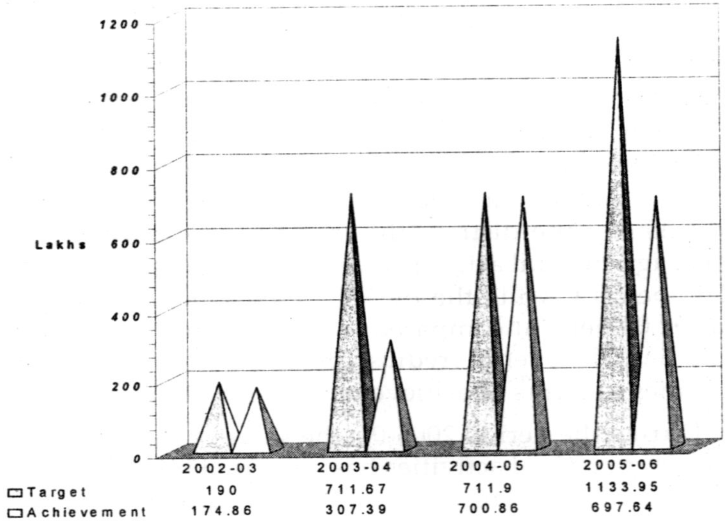

Table 2.5: Purpose-Wise Agricultural Advances

Year	*Direct Finance (Rs. In lakh)*	*Loans for Allied Activities*	*Total*
<u>2002-2003</u>			
Target	190 (52.63)	171 (47.37)	361
Achievement	174.86 (60.11)	116.02 (939.89)	290.88
% Achievement	92.03	67.85	80.58
<u>2003-2004</u>			
Target	711.67 (85.49)	120.83 (14.51)	832.5
Achievement	307.39 (78.65)	83.45 (21.35)	390.84
% Achievement	43.19	69.06	46.95
<u>2004-2005</u>			
Target	711.90 (84.58)	129.82 (15.42)	841.72
Achievement	700.86 (92.01)	60.88 (7.99)	761.74
% Achievement	98.45	46.90	90.05

2005-2006			
Target	1133.95 (82.24)	244.45 (17.73)	1378.84
Achievement	697.64 (86.60)	107.93 (13.40)	805.57
% Achievement	61.52	44.15	58.42
2002-2006 (Over all)			
Target	2747.52 (80.48)	666.10 (19.52)	3414.06
Achievement	1880.75 (83.62)	368.28 (16.38)	2249.03
% Achievement	68.45	55.29	65.88

Note: Figures in parentheses indicate the percentage to total

Source: NABARD, Kolkata, 2002-2006

2.6 Term-Wise Composition of Direct Advances

The direct agricultural advances may be divided into two broad categories : (1) crop loans and (2) term loans. The repayment period of crop loans is one year which may be extended upto 18 months. The repayment period of term loans varies from 3 to 10 years.[3]

Term-wise composition of direct agricultural finance is presented in Table 2.6. From the table we find that the direct finance to agriculture has increased in all the years except 2003. Between 2001 and 2006, total direct finance has increased from Rs 34.16 lakhs to Rs 697.64 lakhs registering an increase of 1942 percent in 2006 over the base year. By type of advances, the growth rate is the highest (more than 22 times) in the case of term loans, followed by crop loans (20 times). From another angle we can see that the share of crop loans in total direct finance has decreased from 76.73 percent in 2001 to 74.39 percent in 2006 accounting for2.34 percent decrease over the base year. As against this, the share of term loans has increased from 23.27 percent to 25.61 percent, over the same period. When the percent change in crop loans is worked out it is seen that the crop loans are found, but its magnitude is much less than that of term loans in 2006 over the base year. This may be partly due to increasing importance of farm mechanization and land develop ment in term loans. As a result the variation is too much in term loans in comparison to crop loans. The head-wise direct advances is shown in Figure 2.4.

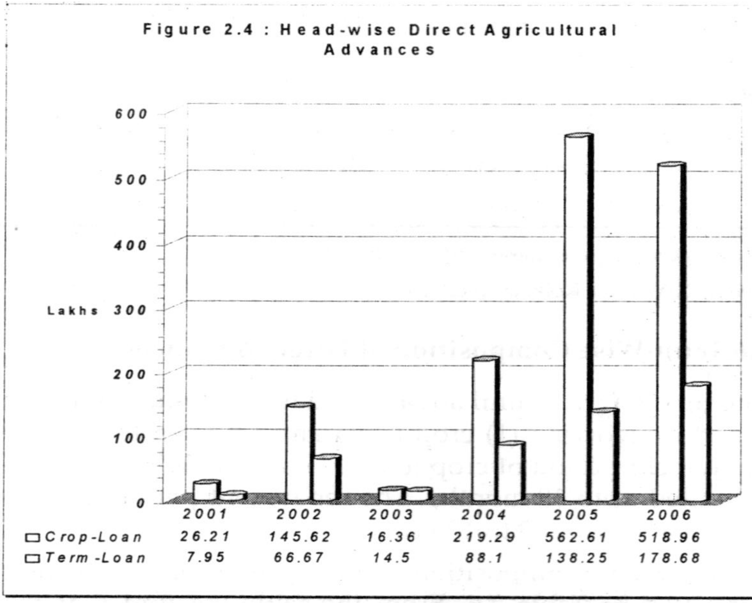

Figure 2.4 : Head-wise Direct Agricultural Advances

Table 2.6: Composition of Direct Finance

Year	*Crop Loan*	*Term Loan*	*Total*	*% of Crop Loan in Total Direct Finance*	*% of Term Loan in Total Direct Finance*
2001	26.21	7.95	34.16	76.73	23.27
2002	145.62	66.67	212.29	68.60	31.41
2003	160.36	14.50	174.86	91.71	8.29
2004	219.29	88.10	307.39	71.34	28.66
2005	562.61	138.25	700.86	80.27	19.72
2006	518.96	178.68	697.64	74.39	25.61

Source: District Credit Plan, Jalpaiguri, 2001-2006

2.6.1 *Borrowal Accounts Under Direct Finance*

Number of borrowal accounts show the popularity of the bank among the borrowers for lending purpose. The UBKGB has not achieved a commendable success in this regard.

The number of borrowal account is shown in Table 2.7. From the table it is clear that the number of Borrowal accounts of UBKGB have been increasing at a constant rate (column 3) between 2001 to 2003 but since 2004 the variation in accounts has decreased. We find also from the chain base index number that the borrowal accounts have increased only 12 percent in 2006 over the base period. It means that the borrowers have not accepted this bank fully as their money- lender and they are not getting full advantage of agricultural credit facilities according their needs. Between 2001 to 2006 the average increase per year in these accounts come to only 292 accounts.

Table 2.7: Quantum of Borrowal Accounts of Direct Finance

Year	*No. of Accounts*	*Variation in Previous Year*	*Chain Base Index No. of Accounts*
2001	1072	1072	100
2002	2097	1025	195.62
2003	2583	1080	123.18
2004	3568	985	138.13
2005	3879	311	108.72
2006	4341	462	111.91

Source: Data Supplied By Head Office, UBKGB, Cooch Behar, 2001-2006

2.6.2 *Size of Borrowal Accounts*

Size of borrowal accounts refers to the amount which a borrower borrows from the bank. The average size of borrowal accounts4 is shown in Table 2.8.

From table 2.8 we find that the average amount of direct agricultural loans per account has increased from Rs 3.19 in 2001 to Rs 16.07 in 2006 registering an increase of 403.73 percent in2006 over the base period. By type of account, over the same period, the size of crop loans has increased from Rs. 3.47per account to Rs. 17.80, that of term loan from Rs. 2.51 to Rs.12.54 per account. The reason for large increase in average amount of crop loans per account may be due to the fact that the bank is giving more importance in the development of crop output by way of financing more credit.

Table 2.8 : Average Size of Accounts of Direct Finance

Type of Loan	*2001*		*2006*	
	No. of Accounts ('000)	*Amount per Account (Rs)*	*No. of Accounts ('000)*	*Amount per Account*
Crop Loans	755	3.47	2916	17.80
Term Loans	317	2.51	1425	12.54
Total	1072	3.19	4341	16.07

Source: Different Annual Reports of UBKGB, Jalpaiguri, 2001-2006.

2.7 Determinants of Crop Loans

On the basis of three years value (2003-2005) of cropping intensity and total cropped area as determining factors of short-term loan, linear and log-linear equations are worked out as below in equations (1) and (2).

(1) Linear Model

$$Y = a + b_1 x_1$$

Y = short-term loans (in Rs.)

x_1 = Total cropped area (in 000 hectare. Area)

Log-linear Model

$$\text{Log } Y = \log a + b_1 \log x_1$$

(2) Linear Model

$$Y = a + b_2 x_2$$

$$\text{Log } Y = \log a + b_2 \log x_2$$

x_2 = cropping intensity

Result

I. Crop Loans and Total Cropped Area (TCA)

In order to asses the extent of the impact of explanatory variables on short-term loans, linear and the regression co-efficients are presented in table 2.9

Table 2.9: Regression Analysis, Linear Function, Dependent variable-Crop loans (Period 2003-2005)

Description		Independent Variable (X1)
Regression Co-efficient		0.3486*
Intercept	-65611	
F-Value	3.46	
R2	0.643	

*significant at 20 percent level.

Table 2.10: Regression Analysis, Log-linear Function, Dependent Variable-Crop Loans

Description		Independent Variable (X1)
Regression Co-efficient		98573.2*
Intercept	1E+o6	
F-Value	2.69	
R2	0.574	

*significant at 24 percent level.

In the linear as well as log-linear forms, the total cropped are turns out to be significant at 20 percent level in linear equation and at 24 percent level in log-linear equation. The value of R2 is 643 for linear and.574 for log-linear functions. This indicates that TCA explains 64 (Linear) and 57 percent (log-linear) variations in crop loans. Thus the regression co-efficients are found to be positive and significant in both functions, implying thereby that the TCA has a direct and positive bearing on the crop loans advanced by the UBKGB in the district.

II. Crop Loans and Cropping Intensity

Cropping intensity turns out also to be significant for exogeneous variable in case of crop loans. The Linear function gives a better fit since the value of R2 is 0.95 (Table 2.11).

Table 2.11 : Regression Analysis, Linear Function Dependent variable - Crop loans, period 2003-05

Description		Independent Variable (X1)
Regression Co-efficient		0.0925*
Intercept	-110292	
F-Value	34.98	
R2	0.95	

*significant at 3 percent level.

Table 2.12 : Regression Analysis, Log- Linear Function

Description		Independent Variable X2
Regression Co-efficient		158755*
Intercept	- 2E+06	
F- Value	30.30	
R2	0.94	

*significant at 3 percent level.

The analysis shows that cropping intensity is the most important variable that affects the credit requirements. TCA is the second important variable responsible for changes in crop loans. Thus for an increase in cropping intensity and TCA, more crop loans facilities are needed. It requires revamping of crop loans for agricultural sector in the district.

2.8 Agricultural Credit, Total Cropped Area and Bank Deposit

In order to examine the relationship in between the agricultural credit, total cropped area and bank deposit, a multiple regression technique based on the OLS method, for the period 2002-05 has been employed. The choice of variables and specification of the model are discussed below :

$Y = f(x_1, x_2)$

Y = Agricultural advances (in Rs.) (AA)

X_1 = Total cropped area (in 000 hectares) (TCA)

x_2 = Bank deposits (in Rs.) (BD)

As per the available empirical evidence, multi-colinearity is not a serious problem in our estimates5. Linear function has been worked out.

Linear Model

$Y = a + b_1x_1 + b_2x_2$

Result :

Regression co-efficients of independent variables estimated through multiple regression analysis along with t-values and co-efficient of multiple determination (R2) for agricultural credit are given in table 2.13

Table 2.13 : Dependent variable - Agricultural credits, Period 2002-2005

Variable	*Co-efficient*	*Standard Error*	*t- Value*	*R^2*	*R*
TCA	- 0.117**	0.180	-0.648	0.962	0.981
BD	- 0.115*	0.039	2.936		

*significant at 20% probability level

** not significant

The linear function gives a better fit since the value of R2 is 0.96. This indicates that 96 percent of the variations in AA are explained by TCA and BD.

The test shows that only bank deposit turns out to be the dominating variable. The relationship between AA and BD is positive and significant at 20 percent level. Whereas the relationship between AA and TCA is negative as well as statistically insignificant. This indicates that the deposit mobilisation exerts substantially greater influence on the agricultural advances as compared to TCA. The regression co- efficient of AA on BD has been found to be +0.115 indicating thereby that 1 percent increase in BD will bring about an increase of 0.115 percent in AA.

2.9 Purpose-Wise Classification of Agricultural Term-Loans

The UBKGB is giving agricultural term-loans under the following heads :

(a) Minor irrigation (MI) which includes shallow tube well, dug well, pump-set etc.

(b) Land development (LD) includes land reclamation, management of waterlogged, seed production and processing, farm development etc.

(c) Farm mechanization (FM) which contains power-tiller, tractor and Agricultural. Implements.

(d) Plantation and Horticulture. (P and H)

With the advent of the new technology in agriculture, the cash requirements to purchase modern inputs are going up perceptibly. Hence to cope with modern technology that crept into agriculture, farmers need adequate agricultural term-loans for the above diversified purposes. The analysis is aimed at examining the extent of flow of agriculture. Term loans from the UBKGB are used for various purposes. The purpose wise classification of agricultural term loans given by the UBKGB is presented in Table 2.14.

Table 2.14 : Purpose-Wise Classification of Agricultural Term-Loans

Purpose	*2001-2002*	*2005-06*	*% change in 2005-06 over 2001-02*
MI	19.26 (28.89)	9.16 (5.13)	-52.44
LD	1.6 (2.40)	18.64 (10.43)	1064
FM	26.71 (40.06)	20.02 (11.20)	-25.05
P and H	4.56 (6.84)	94.35 (52.80)	1969.08
Others	14.54 (21.81)	36.51(20.43)	151.10
All	66.67	178.68	168.01

Source: NABARD, Kolkata, 2001-02 and 2005-06.

Table 2.14 reveals that in 2001-02, farm mechanization was found maximum in Jalpaiguri district (Rs. 26.71) followed by minor irrigation (Rs. 19.26). The term loans on land development was observed minimum followed by plantation and horticulture.

In the case of FM, the rank has down-ward shifted from one to three, witnessing a negative growth rate (-25.05%) over 2001-02, whereas P and H has made an upward shift from 4th to 1st rank but has witnessed an increase of 1969.08 percent. The minor irrigation in the district has downward shifted from two to five witnessing a decrease of -52.44percent over 2001-02.

As regards the proportionate share to total term loans given by the UBKGB, the percentage share of farm mechanisation in total term loans for agricultural purposes was 40.06 percent in 2001-02. It has decreased to 11.20 percent in 2005-06 while the proportionate share of P and H in total agricultural term loans was only 6.84 percent in 2001-02. It has increased markedly to 52.80 percent in 2005-06. Similarly the share of credit for minor irrigation has decreased from 28.89 percent in 2001-02 to 5.13 percent in 2005-06. The share of credit for land development has increased 4 fold during the same period.

Agricultural term-loans for plantation and horticulture have recorded the highest growth rate while the second highest rate of growth is noticed in the case of credit for land development. That is why P and H has become the first important recipient of term loans from the UBKGB in 2005-06. The purpose wise classification of term loans is presented in figure 2.3. Thus from the points of view of agricultural term loans given by the UBKGB, the lion's share of credit has gone to plantation and horticulture and the rest portion has gone to all others. Purpose-wise agricultural term loans is presented in figure 2.5.

2.10 Loans for Allied Activities

Activities allied to agriculture are those which provide added employment and supplement the family income of the cultivators. Such activities include dairying, poultry farming, piggery, fisheries, sheep rearing, storage/market yard etc. The credit disbursed by the UBKGB for allied activities has increased from Rs. 20.78 lakhs in 1998-99 to Rs. 107.93 lakhs in 2005-06. But the share of such loans in total agricultural credit has decreased from 34.09 percent to 13.40 percent over the period.

Figure 2.5: Purpose-wise Classification of Term Loan 2001-02 (Inner Series) and 2005-06 (Outer Series) (Figures in Percentage)

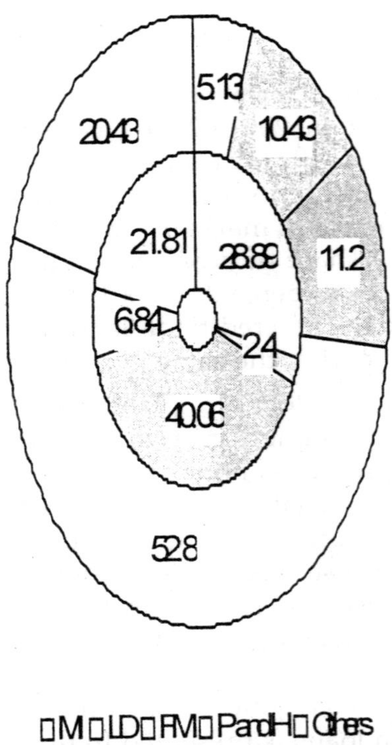

The purpose-wise distribution of agricultural credit for allied activities given by the UBKGB is presented in Table 2.15.

Table 2.15 : Purpose-wise Classification of Agricultural Credit For Allied Activities

Purpose	*1998-99*	*2005-06*	*Percent Change in 2005-06 over 1998-99*
Dairying	12.84 (55.13)	26.99 (25.01)	110.20
Poultry Farming	0.23 (0.99)	8.76 (8.12)	3708.69
SGP units	4.01 (17.22)	23.30 (21.59)	481.05
Fisheries	3.17 (13.61)	6.55 (6.07)	106.62
Others	3.04 (13.05)	42.33 (39.22)	1292.43
Total	23.29	107.93	363.42

Source: District credit Plan, Jalpaiguri 1998-99 and 2005-06

Table 2.15 gives a comprehensive picture of the coverage of UBKGB's advances for allied activities. Activity-wise financing of dairying activity has recorded considerable increase from Rs. 12.48 lakhs in 1999 to Rs. 26.99 lakhs in 2006 registering an increase of 110.20 percent. Poultry farming is an another important allied activity financed by the bank. The UBKGB's loans for such purpose have increased from Rs. 0.23 lakhs in 1999 to Rs. 8.76 lakhs in 2006 which has recorded the growth rate of 3708.69 percent. As regards of UBKGB's advances to fisheries, another important allied activity which has increased more than 2 times from 1999 to 2006 by registering an increase of 106.62 percent. The residuary item 'others', which has markedly increased from Rs. 3.04 lakhs to Rs. 42.33 lakhs during the same period.

As regards proportionate share of credit under such activities, the percentage share credit to total credit for dairying development was the highest. It was 55.13 percent in 1999 and has declined since then to 25.01 percent in 2006 while the percentage share of poultry farming to total agricultural credit has increased from 9.99 percent to about 8.12 percent during the same period. The rank of SGP units has made an upward shift from two to three (from 17.22 percent to 21.59 percent). In the case of fisheries, the percentile share in total agricultural credit has declined from 13.61 percent to 6.07percent during the same period. The rate growth of agricultural credit under these categories made available by the UBKGB is 363.43 percent in 2006 over 1999. Credit for poultry farming has recorded the highest growth rate (3708.69 percent). The second highest growth rate is noticed in the case of other activities i.e. forestry, storage/market yard etc. The purpose-wise classification of agricultural credit for allied activities is presented in Figure 2.6.

Figure 2.6: Purpose-wise classification of Allied Agricultural Advances (Figures in Percentage) Inner Series 1998-99 Outer Series 2005-06

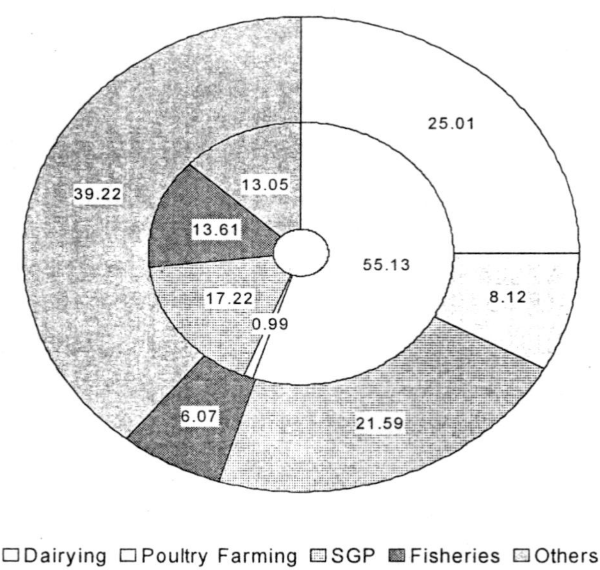

Thus from the point of view of agriculture credit of allied activities given by the UBKGB, the banking operation has taken much care of the cultivators and the bank is trying to give more loans to the farmers for production, marketing of crops, purchase of agriculture implements etc.

2.11 Beneficiary-Wise Flow of Agricultural Credit

The UBKGB that came into being during 1976 in Jalpaiguri district of W.B. is extending credit facilities to a large number of people including SC, ST, minority classes and other backward classes etc. Of the weaker sections, the share of small farmers, marginal farmers and agricultural labourers in the total agricultural Credit disbursement made by the Bank in the district is discussed here. The share of marginal farmers compared to small farmers and agricultural labourers is more during the period 2004-06. The share of agricultural labourers in the total disbursement is significantly lower. This kind of skewed pattern of disbursement among various groups of the weaker sections is found to have emerged possible due to variation in coverage of population under each category.

Table 2.16 : Beneficiary-Wise Flow of Agricultural Credit by the UKGB

(Rs. In Lakh)

Farm Size	*2003-04*		*2004-05*		*2005-06*	
	Amount	*Per head availability*	*Amount*	*Per head availability*	*Amount*	*Per head availability*
SF	12658	98.124	22204	172.12	13290	103.20
MF	15485	397.05	22919	767.15	21695	556.28
AL	1426	7.92	2136	11.87	4886	27.14

Source: District credit plans Jalpaiguri, 2003-06.

Beneficiary-wise classification of credit is shown in table 2.16. Of the total cultivators, the number of small farmers is much more than the number of marginal farmers. In term of disbursement per head, the marginal farmers score reasonably higher followed by the small farmers and agricultural labourers. The agricultural credit made available from the UBKGB to small farmers has increased about 1.05 times during the period 2003.06. While credits available to the marginal farmers and agricultural labourers have increased 1.40 times and 3.43 times respectively during the same period. The rate of growth of agricultural credit in respect of agricultural labourers is the highest (243 percentage) in 2006 over 2003, the second highest growth rate is noticed in the case of Marginal farmers (40percent) and the lowest growth rate of credit is seen in the case of small farmers (4.99percent) over the same period. But in terms of disbursement per head, the marginal farmers appear to be higher than any other group. Thus in terms of disbursement per individual, the marginal farmers seem to have benefited more than any other groups of the weaker sections. But in terms of the growth rate of agricultural credit advanced by the UBKGB, agricultural labourers seem to have been benefited more. Therefore, it is well proved that the UBKGB has been engaged in developing agriculture in the district in general and the agriculturists in particular.

2.12 Caste-Wise Disbursement

By the large, the major chunk of population of the district belonging to weaker sections is constituted by SC, ST and OBC population. The UBKGB is playing a significant role in extending finance to SC, ST and other backward caste population. The general presumption is that the proportion of credit flow to the SC, ST and OBC categories together is much higher than the credit flow to the upper caste people. This is clear from table 2.17. From the table 2.17 it is clear that the UBKGB during 2003-04 sanctioned agricultural loans aggregating Rs. 219.86 lakhs to SC population. This has increased to Rs 4777.51 lakhs in 2005-06 registering an

Table 2.17 : Caste-Wise Distribution of Agricultural Credit

Year	*SC*	*ST*	*OBC*	*Forward caste*	*Total*
2004	219.86	38.05	56.93	76.00	390.84
2005	572.72	48.78	60.28	79.96	761.74
2006	477.51	61.55	163.85	102.66	805.57

Source: District credit Plan, Jalpaiguri, 2004-06.

increase of 61.40 percent. The advances extended by the UBKGB to ST population have increased from Rs. 38.05 lakhs to Rs. 61.55 lakhs during the same period. The growth rate of credit under this category is 61.76 percent in 2006 over 2004. While the amount of loans to the OBC category has increased from Rs. 56.93 lakhs in 2004 to Rs. 163.85 lakhs in 2006, an increase of almost 2.88 times (188 percent). On the otherhand the agricultural credit disbursed by the bank to the upper caste people has increased from Rs. 76 lakhs in 2004 to Rs. 102.66 lakhs in 2006, an increase of almost 35 percent. Thus within the low caste categories of population the credit that flow to backward caste people is relatively more than S.C. and S.T. This observation tends to establish the fact in terms of credit disbursement, the OBC is more favoured than SC and ST. The relatively more bias towards OBC has happened perhaps due to the fact that people belonging to the OBC categories possess more land than the other group of weaker sections viz. SC and ST or the relatively more bias towards OBC may be more accessibility of these sections to the bank. At another level we observe that the credit flows to the SC, ST and OBC category of population together is higher than that of the upper caste people.

2.13 Recovery Performance

From the foregoing analysis it is seen that the UBKGB has recorded considerable progress in advancing loans to agriculture over the period 1999-06. However this cannot be said about its performance at recovery of these agricultural loans. The importance of recovery as an aspect of managing credit operations can hardly be over emphasised as productive use of bank credit mainly depends on how regularly loans are recovered and funds are recycled for further productive uses. The UBKGB like any other RRB has been suffering from the acute problem of poor recovery of advances given by it. On the one hand its resources are limited and deposit mobilisation is poor and on the other hand, poor percentage of recovery makes its resources further poor.

Table 2.18 : Recovery Position of the UBKGB

Year	*Total Advances (Rs in thousand)*	*Total Recovery (Rs in thousand)*	*Recovery Percentage*
2000	6112	2172	35.53
2001	5400	1668	30.88
2002	29088	10033	34.49
2003	20700	6241	30.15
2004	39084	9603	24.57
2005	76174	18845	24.74
2006	80557	20880	25.92

Source: District credit Plans, Jalpaiguri, 2000-06.

From the table 2.18 it is evident that with some insignificant exceptions the recovery percentage has been falling as it has come down from 35.53 percent in 2002 to 24.57 percent in 2004 after that it is being slightly improved as it has been 24.74 percent in 2005 and 25.92 percent in 2006. This shows that the performance of the bank has not been upto the mark on the front of recovery which has hampered the future prospect of the bank. The diagrammatic presentation of recovery position of the bank is given in Figure 2.7. The overview of recovery performance of UBKGB will be dealt with elaborately in chapter 5.

Figure 2.7: Recovery Position of the UBKGB

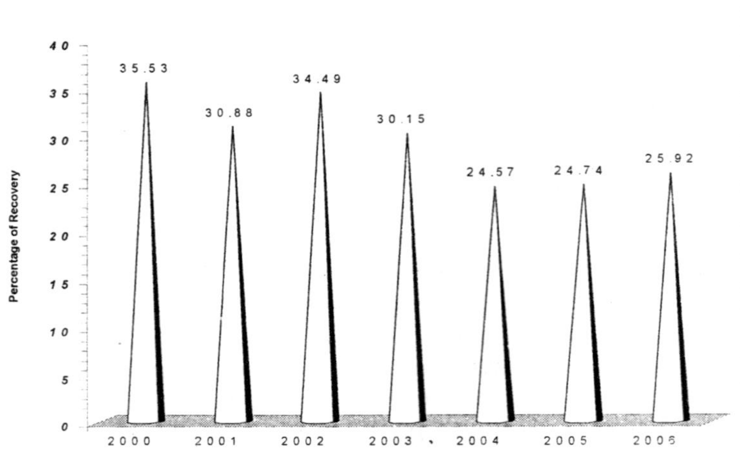

2.14 Comparative Analysis

It will be interesting to compare the performance of UBKGB in agricultural financing with that of Co-operative banks, of the district which are a pioneer agency in this sphere. The comparative analysis is shown with the helpof Table 2.19.

Table 2.19 : Direct Advances to Agriculture by Co-operative Banks and UBKGB- Loans Issued

Year	*Co-operative Banks*			*UBKGB*		
	Crop Loan	*Term Loan*	*Total*	*Crop Loan*	*Term Loan*	*Total*
2001-02	548.32	265.01	813.33	145.62	145.26	290.88
2002-03	619.49	216.61	836.10	160.36	46.64	207
2003-04	548.32	216.61	764.93	345.81	45.03	390.84
2004-05	619.49	479.22	1098.71	598.99	162.75	761.74
2005-06	1616.19	487.93	2104.12	697.64	107.93	805.57

Source: NABARD, Kolkata, 2001-06.

From the Table 2.19 it is evident that the total agricultural loans granted by the co-operative banks have increased 2.59 times being Rs. 2104.12 lakhs in 2006 from Rs. 813.33 lakhs in 2002, whereas those of UBKGB have increased 2.77 times from Rs. 290.88 lakhs to Rs. 805.57 lakhs during the same period.

The break-up of the UBKGB's loans to agriculture shows that its short-term loans to agriculture has recorded a larger growth rate than its term loans. For example, the growth rate of short-term loan to agriculture given by the UBKGB is 379.08 percentage in 2005-06 over 2001-02, while the growth rate of term loans is negative i.e. - 25.70 percent during the same period. Whereas, in the case of co-operative agencies both types of loans have increased more or less at the same rate. It may also be mentioned that like UBKGB and Co-operatives, CBs provide loans, to agriculture in the district. But the total agricultural advances granted by the commercial bank have increased only 1.52 times being Rs. 6045.68 lakhs in 2001-02 to Rs. 920.64 lakhs in 2005-06. This fact proves that in comparison to CBs and Co-operative agencies, the position of agricultural advances in general but short-term loans in particular given by the UBKGB is satisfactory for the downtrodden people in the district..

2.15 Conclusion

It is seen from the above analysis that by and large UBKGB has made a considerable progress in lending to the agricultural sector. Bank loans by way of direct finance to agriculture have increased manifold especially since 1999. On the basis of loaning performance, it may be easily concluded that there has been both quantitative and qualitative growth of agricultural sector of the rural economy with the establishment of the UBKGB branches in different villages of Jalpaiguri district. The UBKGB has also a considerable contribution in agricultural activities as it has been doing better in comparison to the Co-operative banks in the district. But the position of advances can only become optimum when some drastic efforts are made with proper planning.

NOTES AND REFERENCES

1. "Study of Utilisation of Co-operative Loans", Planning Commission, India, 1965.
2. In this present study we have used "term loans". The reason behind this is that only the loans advanced by the UBKGB are classified into short term and term loans.
3. In some cases, the period of term loans may be extended upto 20 years depending on the purpose for which loan is provided.
4. Average size of borrowal account is computed by dividing the total direct agricultural advances in any year by the number of borrowal accounts in that year.
5. If correction co-efficient (r) between a pair of variables is greater than 0.81, The problem of multi-collinearity may arise according to E.O. Heady and J.C. Dhillion as mentioned in the book, "Agricultural Production Function", P.115. But according to L.R.Klein, if the value of multiple correction co-efficient (R) is higher than simple correlation co-efficient (r) then the multi-collinearity should not be considered serious.

3

UBKGB and Credits Needs of Farmers

3.1 Introduction

Farmers require credit for various purposes. This may be both Productive and unproductive. They require credit for conducting agricultural operations, for purchasing agricultural inputs as well as for meeting their consumption needs. An assessment of credit needs of the farmers is not an easy task. But it is a common experience that availability of credit always falls short of requirements with dampening effect on the agricultural operations. Undoubtedly there has been tremendous increase in the availability of credit to the farmers after the expansion of banking institutions in rural areas. Yet the farmers continue to be in the strong grip of the local money lenders due to inadequacy of credit available to the cultivators.

In this present chapter an attempt has been made to assess the credit needs of the farmers. The chapter is divided into five sections. The first section (3.2) presents a socio-economic profile of the borrowers. The second section (3.3) deals with credit requirements of the borrowers and their utilisation. The third section (3.4) examines the time taken by the UBKGB in disbursing loans. The fourth section

(3.5) presents the cost of borrowing credit and the last section (3.6) deals with loss of time and loss wage earnings.

3.2 Socio-Economic Profile of Borrowers

Before examining a detailed investigation of credit, it is desirable to know about the socio-economic characteristics of the borrowers who participated in the survey. Accordingly in the following sections, efforts have been made to throw light on their socio-economic characteristics by using certain general indicators such as farm size family size, age, caste pattern and education.

Farm Size

Table 3.1 shows the occupational pattern and classification of the sample borrowers according to farm-size. Table 3.1 shows that 40 percent of the borrowers are small farmers, 32.5 percent of the borrowers are marginal farmers; 12.5 percent are medium farmers and 15 percent are agricultural labourers. Hence a maximum of 64 borrowers (40 percent) of the borrowers in the sample are loanees in the village having land holding from 2.5 acres to 5 acres.

Table 3.1: Distribution of Borrowers by Farm-size

Farm size	*No. of Borrowers*	*Percentage to Total*
SF	64	40
MF	52	32.5
MF*	20	12.5
AL	24	15
Total	160	100

Source: Field survey, 2006-07 SF = Small farmers
MF = Marginal farmers
MF* = Medium farmers
AL = Agricultural labourers

Family Size

Family size is considered as an important variable in determining the magnitude of funds required to meet consumption need. The judicious use of loan and its repayment depend on the consumption needs of the family. Data presented in table 3.2 show the size of the family of the loanees.

Table 3.2: Family Size

Farm size	*Family Size*			*Total*
	Below3	*3-5*	*Above5*	
SF	-	53	11	64
		(82.81)	(17.19)	(100)
MF	10	38	4	52
	(19.23)	(73.08)	(7.69)	(100)
MF*	12	8	-	20
	(60)	(40)		(100)
AL	8	10	6	24
	(33.33)	(41.67)	(25)	(100)
Total	30	10	21	160
	(18.75)	(68.12)	(13.12)	(100)

Note: Figures in the parentheses indicate percentages.

Source: Field survey, 2006-07.

Table 3.2 shows that in the case of small farmers of 64 borrowers, 53 have a family size of above 5 persons. 10 borrowers (19.23 percent) in the case of marginal farmers, 12 borrowers (60 percent) in the case of medium farmers and 8 borrowers (33.33 percent) have a family size below 3 persons. A majority of 38 borrowers (73.08 percent) in the case of marginal farmers have a family size of 3 to 5 persons and 10 borrowers (41.67 percent) of agricultural labourers class have a family size of 3 to 5 persons. Overall, in the sample, a majority of borrowers i.e., 68.12 percent have a family size of 3-5 members. About 18.75 percent of the sample borrowers have a family size below 3 members and 13.12 percent have a family size above 5 members.

Age

Table 3.3 shows the age structure of the family of the respondents.

Table 3.3: Age Structure of the Family of Respondents

Farm Size	*Distribution of family of respondents*					
	15-40		*40-65*		*Total*	
	Male	*Female*	*Male*	*Female*	*Male*	*Female*
SF	20	12	28	4	48	16
	(20.67)	(75)	(58.33)	(25)	(100)	(100)
MF	22	8	16	10	38	18
	(57.89)	(44.44)	(42.11)	(55.56)	(100)	(100)
MF*	-	-	20	-	20	-
			(100)		(100)	
AL	10	6	6	2	15	8
	(62.50)	(75)	(37.50)	(25)	(100)	(100)
Total	52	26	70	16	122	42
	(42.62)	(61.90)	(57.38)	(38.10)	(100)	(100)

Figures in the parentheses indicate percentages.

Source: Field survey, 2006-07.

Table 3.3 shows that out of the total of 122 males, 42.62 percent of males are in the age group of 15 to 40 years and the rest i.e 57.38 percent are above 40 years of age. Out of 42 females, 61.90 percent are in the age group of 15 to 40 years and the rest 38.10 percent are above 40 years of age. In small farmers category, out of 62 borrowers, 41.67 percent of males are in the age-group of 15-40 years and the rest i.e., 58.33 percent males are above 40 years of age, 75 percent are above 40 years of age. Out of 52 borrowers in marginal farmers category, 57.89 percent males are in the age group of 15-40 years of age and the rest i.e., 42.11 percent are above 40 years of age, 44.44 percent females are in the age group of 15-40 years and 55.66 percent females are above 40 years of age and out of 24 borrowers of agricultural labourers category, 62.50 percent males and 75 percent females are in the age-group of 15-40 years and the rest i.e.,

37.50 percent males and 25 percent females are above 40 years of age.

Caste

Table 3.4 shows the caste pattern of the respondents included in the sample.

Table 3.4: Caste Pattern of the Respondents

Types of farmers	*Scheduled caste*	*Scheduled Tribes*	*Other Backward Caste*	*General Caste*	*Total*
SF	32 (50)	17 (26.56)	13 (20.31)	2 (3.12)	64 (100)
MF	20 (38.46)	13 (25)	14 (26.92)	5 (9.62)	52 (100)
MF*	12 (60)	-	-	8 (40)	20 (100)
AL	8 (33.33)	12 (50)	4 (16.67)	-	24 (100)
Total	72 (45)	42 (26.25)	31 (19.38)	15 (9.38)	160 (100)

Figures in the parentheses indicate percentages.

Source: Field Survey 2006-07.

From table 3.4 it is observed that majority of the borrowers particularly that of small, marginal and medium farmers belong to scheduled caste. Out of 160 sample borrowers, 45 percent belong to scheduled caste, 26.25 percent belong to scheduled tribes, 19.38 percent belong to other backward caste and the rest i.e., 9.38 percent belong to general caste. Out of 116 borrowers in the sample comprising of small and marginal farmers 52 borrowers (88.46 percent) belong to scheduled caste.

Most of the borrowers belonging to scheduled caste are medium farmers. Out of 15 borrowers of general caste in the sample, 8 borrowers i.e., 40 percent are medium farmers. 7 borrowers i.e., 12.74 percent belong to small and marginal farmers. Further no borrowers under agricultural labourer class is found from general caste. Thus most of the small, marginal and medium farmers belong to scheduled caste and most of the agricultural labourers belong to scheduled tribes.

Education

Education is an absolute necessity for the purpose of meaningful participation of the rural people in development activities. It is believed that an educated person can make better use of credit and thus generate a surplus enough to repay the loan1. Table 3.5 presents information on the education levels status of the sample borrowers.

Table 3.5: Education-wise Distribution of Sample Borrowers

	Literacy Level			
	Illiterate	*Primary*	*Secondary and Above*	*Total*
SF	10 (15.62)	30 (46.88)	24 (37.5)	64 (100)
MF	30.(57.69)	20 (38.46)	2 (3.85)	52 (100)
MF*	8 (40)	10 (50)	2 (10)	20 (100)
AL	19 (79.17)	3 (12.5)	2 (8.33)	24 (100)
Total	67 (41.88)	63 (39.38)	30 (18.74)	160 (100)

Figures in the parentheses represent percentages

Source: Field Survey, 2006-07.

Occupation

An individual's occupation determines the stability of his earnings which in turn influences the repayment behaviour of the borrowers. Table 3.6 presents a distribution of borrowers by occupation.

The table reveals that agriculture is the mainstay for 75.62 percent of the borrowers. 24.38 percent of the borrowers are engaged in business activity. 48.76 percent of the small farmers are engaged in agricultural and 12.82 percent in business activity. 34.71 percent of small farmers are exclusively engaged in agriculture and 25.64 percent in business activity while 16.53 percent of medium farmers are engaged only in agriculture. Business activity is the main occupation for 61.54 percent of the borrowers under agricultural labourers.

3.3 Credit Needs of the Borrowers and Their Fulfilment

The rural credit institutions are engaged in providing credit facilities to the weakers sections of the society. But if the borrowers are provided inadequate funds to run their activities, it may render their activities unviable. Thus the success of the activities undertaken by the borrowers depends on the provision of adequate financial assistance. If the borrowers do not have adequate funds to invest along with borrowed amount, it may lead to diversion of borrowed amount from productive purposes to non-productive purposes. In keeping with this view during field survey the informations regarding credit required and credit actually obtained have been colleted and analysed to assess the shortage of funds. The overall credit needs of the borrowers and shortage of fund is presented in table 3.6.

Table 3.6: Farm-Wise Distribution of Occupation of Sample Borrowers

Farm size	*Agriculture*	*%age to total*	*Business*	*%age to total*
SF	59	48.76	5	12.82
MF	42	34.71	10	25.64
MF*	20	16.53	-	-
AL	-		24	61.54
Total	121	100	39	100

Source: Field Survey, 2006-07

Table 3.7 shows that the mean credit requirement of the farmers in the six selected village is Rs. 24688.50 and the mean credit disbursed by UBKGB is Rs. 16405.50. This represents that 66.45 percent of the credit requirements of the farmers has been fulfilled by UBKGB. Therefore, 33.55 percent of the credit requirement of the borrowers is not met by UBKGB. It is further noticed from the table that the percentages of credit shortage is comparatively high in the case of small farmers (79.91percent) and lowest in the case of agricultural labourers (23.32 percent). Only 20.09 percent of the credit needs of small farmers is satisfied by UBKGB. In the case of marginal farmers, shortage of credit as percentage of credit requirements is only 22.74 percent representing 77.26 percent of the credit is met by UBKGB. Hence it is concluded that granting of inadequate amount of credit is a common phenomenon in all categories of borrowers in the sample area.

Table 3.7: Credit Needs of the Farmers

Farm Size	*No. of farmers*	*Mean amount (in Rs)*		*Mean shortage of funds (D-S)*	*Shortage of fund as % of demand for credit*
		Demand for credit(D)	*Supply of credit (S)*		
SF	64	17940.62	14335.94	3604.68	79.91
MF	52	19565.38	14372.69	4231.16	26.54
MF*	20	74250	36500	42250	50.84
AL	24	12428.08	9583.33	1232.09	23.32
Total	160	24688.56	16405.50	8283.06	33.55

Source: Field survey, 2006-07

3.3.1 Credit Gap under Different Blocks

Detailed information on credit requirement, supply of credit and percentage of shortage of fund to credit requirement are analysed in six selected villages under different blocks in the forth-coming analysis. Data presented in table 3.7 show the extent to which credit needs of the borrowers are met by UBKGB. It is apparent from the figures that 33.55 percent of the credit needs of the borrowers have not been met by UBKGB.

Table 3.8: Credit Needs and Shortage of Funds

Block	*Supply of credit(S)*	*Mean amount (in Rs)*		*Shortage of fund as %age of demand for credit*
		Demand for credit (D)	*(D – S)*	
Maynaguri Churabhandar and Husludanga	15386.79	24540.94	9154.15	37.30
Rajganj Kaluarbari and Mogha Para	18176.98	23462.26	5285.28	22.53
Jalpaiguri Choudhuri Para and Denguajhar	15666.67	26037.04	1037.37	39.85
Total	16405.50	24688.56	8283.06	33.55

Source: Field Survey, 2006-07.

From Table 3.8 it is found that the shortage of funds is comparatively high in the selected villages under Jalpaiguri Sadar (39.83 percent) and lowest in the selected villages under Rajganj block (22.53 percent). This represents that 60.17 percent of credit requirement in the selected a villages Jalpaiguri Sadar block has been met by UBKGB, whereas 77.47 percent of credit requirement of the borrowers in the selected villages under Rajgang block has been satisfied by UBKGB.

Table 3.9 shows the shortage of funds of sample borrowers in the selected villages under Maynaguri block. From table 3.8 it is found that no significant disparity is found between marginal farmers and medium farmers in the selected villages under Maynaguri block. The percentages as shortage of funds are 47.68 and 47.25 for marginal farmers and medium farmers respectively. Compared to marginal and medium farmers, the small farmers in the selected villages under Maynaguri Block are in a better position with a shortage of 17.54 percent in credit and a mean shortage of only Rs. 2736.36 per farmer. Overall, the credits disbursed by UBKGB seem to have benefited more to the small farmers and agricultural labourers than the medium and marginal farmers in the selected village under Maynaguri block.

Table 3.9: Shortage of Credit of Sample Borrowers in the Selected Villages under Maynaguri Block

Farm size	*Mean amount (in Rs)*		*(D - S)*	*Shortage of credit*
	Demand for credit (D)	*Supply of credit (S)*		*as %age of credit requirement*
SF	15600	12863.64	2736.36	17.54
MF	25087.50	13125	11962.50	47.68
MF*	75833.33	40000	35833.33	47.25
AL	11230	9166.67	2063.33	18.37
Total	24540.94	15386.79	9154.15	37.30

Source: Field Survey, 2006-07.

Data Presented in Table 3.10 shows shortage of credits of sample borrowers in the selected villages under Jalpaiguri sadar. From table 3.9 it is apparent that 39.83 percent of the credit needs of the borrowers have not been satisfied by UBKGB in the selected villages under Jalpaiguri Sadar block. The percentage of credit gap is very low for marginal farmers. Only 3.59 percent of the credit requirements of marginal farmers have not been met by the bank. The inadequacy of funds has been the highest for the medium size farmers (66.56 percent) followed by small farmers (31.71 percent) and agricultural labourers (11.41percent) respectively. The wide variation among the borrowers lends credence to the belief that the type of activity and the level of adequacy of the loan have some sort of correlation.

Table 3.10: Shortage of Credits of Sample Borrowers in the Selected Villages under Jalpaiguri Sadar

Farm size	*Mean amount (in Rs)*		*(D - S)*	*Shortage of funds as %age of credit requirement*
	Demand for credit (D)	*Supply of credit (S)*		
SF	22352.94	15264.71	7088.23	31.71
MF	13304.35	12826.09	478.26	3.59
MF*	104666.66	35000	69666.66	66.56
AL	11500	10187.50	1312.50	11.41
Total	26037.04	15666.67	78545.65	39.83

Source: Field Survey, 2006-07

Table 3.11 displays the shortage of funds of the borrowers in the selected villages under Rajgang block. From the table 3.11 it is apparent that small farmers have an average shortage of Rs. 2000 representing 11.76 percent of the credit requirements. Whereas the beneficiaries under marginal farmer categories have faced a credit deficiency of 21.81 percent (Rs. 5201) and medium farmers 30.35 percent (Rs. 15250). Thus the small farmers in the selected villages under Rajganj block are in a better position. The diagrammatic presentation of credit gap is given in Figure 3.1.

Table 3.11: Statement Showing Shortage of Funds of the Borrowers in Rajganj Block

Farm size	*Mean amount (in Rs)*		*(D - S)*	*Shortage of funds as %age of credit requirement*
	Demand for credit (D)	*Supply of credit (S)*		
SF	17000	15000	2000	11.76
MF	23846	18645	5201	21.81
MF*	50250	35000	15250	30.35
AL	15214	9429	5785	38.02
Total	23462.26	18176.98	5285.28	22.53

Source: Field Survey, 2006-07.

Thus we see that loans advanced by UBKGB are inadequate for the activities undertaken by the beneficiaries. Village-wise analysis shows that the beneficiaries in Jalpaiguri sader have faced a high credit deficiency of 39.83 percent of their requirements and the marginal farmers in this block are in a better position compared to other category of farmers. Hence the hypothesis that "the amount of credit given to borrowers is not adequate to run the activities" is accepted. This inadequacy of supply of funds by UBKGB as per need of borrowers has compelled the borrowers to borrow funds from local money lenders and gramin baniyas at a greater interest.

3.4 Time Taken by UBKGB in Disbursing Loans

The success of an activity undertaken by the borrowers depends not only on adequate supply of credit, it equally depends on the availability of credit at the right time. If the bank takes enough time to sanction and disburse the credit, the cost of the activity must increase. This results in erosion of anticipated benefits of the borrowers due to cost escalation. Undue delay in granting credit is, therefore, tantamount to denial of credit. Due to undue delay in getting credit, the borrowers are forced to borrow money from the local money lenders for meeting their urgent needs at a grater interest.

Table 3.12: Statement Showing Delayed Disbursement of Loan in the Selected Villages in the District

Time taken (in days)	*No. of borrowers*	*Percentage to total*
Upto 7	108	67.50
8-14	46	28.75
15-30	6	3.75
Total	160	100

Source: Field Survey, 2006-07.

For this purpose during field survey the beneficiaries were asked to state the time taken in getting credit to find out whether the borrowers have to wait for a long period of time to get credit. The time taken by the bank in sanctioning credit is presented in table 3.12.

From table 3.12 we find that of the 160 borrowers above 67 percent have got loan from the bank within 7 days. Of the remaining 32.5 percent borrowers, 28.75 percent have waited from 8 to 14 days to get credit and 3.75 percent have got loan within 15 to 30 days. The UBKGB has taken on an average 6.37 days in sanctioning loan.

Table 3.13: Time Taken to Obtain the Loan after Filling the Application in Different Blocks

Time Taken (in days)	*Rajganj Block*	*Maynaguri Block*	*Jalpaiguri Sadar Block*	*Total*
	Kaluarbari and Mogha Para	*Churabhander and Husludanga*	*Choudhuri Para and Denguajhar*	
Up to 7	35(66.04)	29(54.72)	44(81.48)	108(67.50)
8-14	14(26.41)	22(41.51)	10(18.52)	46(28.75)
15-30	4(7.55)	2(3.77)	-	6(3.75)
Total	53(100)	53(100)	54(100)	160(100)

Figures in the parentheses indicate percentages.

Source: Field Survey, 2006-07.

3.4.1 Block-wise Time Lag in Getting Credit

Block-wise analysis (table 3.13) shows that percentage of borrowers who have got loan within 7 days is the highest (81.48 percent) in the villages under Jalpaiguri sadar block followed by Rajganj block (66.04 percent) and Maynaguri block (54.72 percent) respectively. It is very interesting to see that no borrower has waited for more than 15 days to get the loan in Jalpaiguri sadar block whereas 7.55 percent of the borrowers have waited for more than 15 days in Rajganj block followed by Maynaguri block (3.77 percent). The UBKGB has taken 8 to 14 days for 41.51 percent of the borrowers in Maynaguri block followed in descending order by Rajgang block (26.41 percent) and

Jalpaiguri sadar block (18.52 percent). The village-wise mean time taken between the date of application and the date of final disbursement varies from a high of 7.3 days in the selected villages under Maynaguri block to 7 days under Rajganj block and to a low of 5 days under Jalpaiguri sadar.

3.4.2 Farm Size-Wise Delayed Disbursement of Loans

From the table 3.14 it is clear that a large proportion of borrowers under small farmer category (44.83 percent) have got loan from UBKGB within 7 days in Maynaguri block compared to those for marginal farmers (37.59 percent), medium farmers (17.24 percent) and agricultural labourer categories (10.34 percent). In the case of marginal farmers 75 percent of the borrowers have waited for more than 15 days to receive loan. The corresponding percentage in case of small farmer categories is 25. The UBKGB in Maynaguri block has taken on an average 7.09 days for small farmers, 9.41 days for marginal farmers, 4.75 days for medium farmers and 8.5 days for agricultural labourers to grant loan. Thus we can conclude that medium farmers are in a better position to receive loan compared to other category of farmers in Maynaguri block.

Table 3.14: Farm Size-wise Time Taken to Obtain the Loan after Filling the Application in Maynaguri Block

Time Taken	*Farm Size*				*Total*
	SF	*MF*	*MF**	*AL*	
Up to 7	13(59.09)	8(50)	5(83.33)	3(33.33)	29(54.72)
8-14	8(36.36)	5(31.25)	1(16.67)	6(66.67)	20(37.74)
15-30	1(4.54)	3(18.75)	-	-	4(7.55)
Total	22(100)	16(100)	6(100)	9(100)	53(100)

Figures in the parentheses indicate percentages.

Source: Field Survey, 2006-07.

Table 3.15 reveals that in Rajganj block 69.23 percent of the borrowers under marginal farmer categories have received loans within 7 days from the date of application and another 30.77 percent of the borrowers under this category have waited for 7 days to obtain loans and out of the remaining 40.91 percent of borrowers, 36.36 percent have taken 8 to 14 days and 4.54 percent of the borrowers have taken more than 15 days to receive the loan. A larger proportion of the borrowers under medium farmer category (50 percent) have been able to get loans within 7 days and another 50 percent borrowers have taken 8 to 30 days to get the loan. From table 3.14 we can find out that the average time taken by UBKGB in granting credit in Rajganj block is the lowest (5.8 days) for marginal farmer category and it is the highest (10.12 days) in the case of medium farmer category.

Table 3.15: Farm Size-Wise Delayed Disbursement of Loan in the Selected Villages under Rajganj Block

Time Taken (in days)	*SF*	*MF*	*MF**	*AL*	*Total*
Up to 7	16(64)	9(69.23)	4(50)	2(18.57)	31(58.49)
8-14	7(28)	4(30.77)	2(25)	5(71.43)	18(33.96)
15-30	2(8)	-	2(25)	-	4(7.55)
Total	25(100)	13(100)	8(100)	7(100)	53(100)

Figures in the parentheses indicate percentages.

Source: Field Survey, 2006-07.

Table 3.16 present farm size-wise delayed disbursement of loan in Jalpaiguri sadar. From table 3.16 it is noticed that most of the borrowers (82.35 percent) under small farmer category have received loan from UBKGB within 7 days and remaining 17.65 percent have waited for 8 to 14 days to obtain loan. Under marginal farmer categories, majority of the borrowers (73.91 percent) have been able to receive loan within 7 days and under medium farmer category 66.67 percent have received loan within 7 days under agricultural labourer class we find that 62.50 percent of the borrowers have waited for 8 to 14 days to receive loans. The farm-wise mean time lag in Jalpaiguri block in getting credit varies farm a high of 15.31 days for agricultural labourers to 6.5 days for marginal framers, 6 days for medium framers and to a low of 4.8 days for small framers respectively. The diagrammatic presentation of time lag in obtaining credit is given in Figure 3.2.

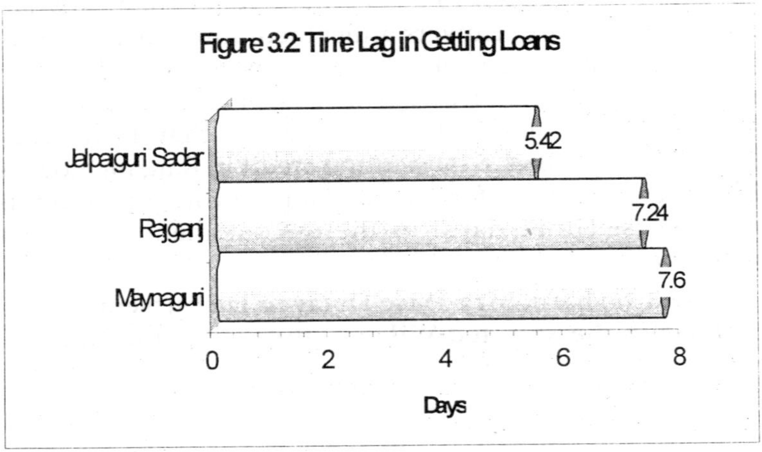

Table 3.16: Farm Size-Wise Delayed Disbursement of Loan in the Selected Villages under Jalpaiguri Sadar

Time Taken (in days)	*SF*	*MF*	*MF**	*AL*	*Total*
Up to 7	14(82.35)	17(83.91)	4(66.67)	-	34(64.82)
8-14	3(17.65)	4(17.39)	2(933.33)	5(62.5)	14(25.92)
15-30	-	2(8.70)	-	3(37.5)	5(9.26)
Total	17(100)	23(100)	6(100)	8(100)	54(100)

Figures in the parentheses indicate percentages.

Source: Field Survey, 2006-07.

The above analysis reveals that sanctioning of loans is a time consuming process and the borrowers had to visit the bank offices several times for clearing the whole procedure. From village-wise analysis under different blocks we see that the delayed receipt of loan is comparatively higher in Maynaguri Block (7.3 days) and lower in Jalpaiguri sadar (5 days). Farm size-wise analysis shows that delay in granting loan is the greatest in the case of marginal farmers (9.41 days) in Maynaguri block and it is the highest in the case of agricultural labourers in Rajganj block (10 days). The delay in granting credit is also the highest (15.31 days) in the case of agricultural labourers in Jalpaiguri sadar. Hence the hypothesis is that "delayed in sanctioning credit" is accepted.

3.5 Cost of Borrowing Credit

It is generally believed that for smooth functioning of an activity undertaken by the borrowers, the credit should be available at the minimum cost. If the cost of borrowing is high, credit availed by the borrowers must be of smaller size. Which in turn affects the viability of the activity due to shortage of credit. The borrowers incur expenditure at various stages from the beginning of filling of application to the date of final disbursement to fulfil various procedural formalities[2]. In our present analysis the cost of borrowing credit consists of stamp duty, processing fees, photograph, essential xerox copies, insurance cost, transport cost, searching fees and subscription to "Farmers' Club". In this study we have tried to calculate the cost of borrowing to find whether the borrowers would be able to tolerate it or not.

3.5.1 Farm Size-Wise Cost of Credit

The table 3.17 presents farm size-wise cost of borrowing credit of the borrowers in the selected villages under different blocks. Table 3.16 shows that borrowers on an average have incurred Rs. 426 as borrowing cost which is equivalent to 2.60 percent of the average credit availed. In the sample area the borrowers under medium farmers category have incurred the highest average borrowing cost of Rs. 550 which is equivalent to 1.51 percent of the average credit obtained. The borrowers under agricultural labourer category have spent the lowest cost of borrowing of Rs. 369 and this amount is equivalent to 3.85 percent of the amount of loan they have obtained. While viewing the cost of borrowing as a proportion of credit obtained, the study reveals that the cost in percentage terms decreases as the amount of credit availed increases. The high percentage (3.85) of borrowing cost of the agricultural labourer class may be due to the small size of individual loan availed therein.

Table 3.17: Farm Size-Wise Cost of Credit

Farm size	*No. of borrowers*	*Mean cost of credit (Rs.)*	*Mean credit supplied (Rs.)*	*Cost of borrowing as % of credit availed*
SF	64	425	14336	2.96
MF	52	405	14373	2.82
MF*	20	550	36500	1.51
AL	24	369	9583	3.85
Total	160	426	16406	2.60

Source: Field Survey, 2006-07

3.5.2 Cost of Credit under Different Blocks

Table 3.18 presents village-wise distribution of cost of credit under different blocks. Table 3.18 shows that the borrowers in Rajganj block have compelled to spend substantial amounts to obtain loan. The average cost of credit in Rajganj block is Rs. 495 which is equal to 2.72 percent of the average credit availed. The average cost of credit is the lowest in Jalpaiguri sadar which is equal to Rs. 359.26 representing 2.29 percent of the average credit availed.

Table 3.18: Village-Wise Classification of Cost of Credit under Different Blocks

Village	*No. of borrowers*	*Mean cost of credit (Rs.)*	*Mean credit supplied (Rs.)*	*Cost of borrowing as % of credit supplied*
Rajganj	53	495	18177	2.72
Kaluarbari and Mogha Para				

Maynaguri	53	425	15387	2.76
Churabhander and Husludanga				
Jalpaiguri	54	359.26	15667	2.29
Choudhuri Para and Denguajhar				
Total	160	426	16406	2.60

Source: Field Survey, 2006-07.

Let us now see the farm size-wise cost of credit in each block. Farm size-wise cost of credit in Rajganj Block is presented in Table 3.19. Table 3.19 depicts that the borrowers under small farmer category have spent the lowest percent of the average credit availed. Where the borrowers under medium farmer category have incurred the highest average cost of credit of Rs. 952 which is equivalent to 2.71 percent of the amount of loan they obtained. The borrowers under marginal farmer category and agricultural labourer class have spent Rs. 440 and Rs. 325 respectively as borrowing cost which represent 2.36 and 5.57 percent respectively of the loan availed.

Table 3.19: Distribution of Cost of Credit among the Farmers in the Selected Villages under Rajganj Block

Type of Farmers	*No. of borrowers*	*Mean cost of credit (Rs.)*	*Mean credit supplied (Rs.)*	*Cost of borrowing as % of credit availed*
SF	25	425	15000	2.83
MF	13	440	18645	2.36
MF*	8	952	35000	2.72
AL	7	325	9429	3.45
Total	53	495	18177	2.72

Source: Field Survey, 2006-07.

Table 3.20 presents the farm size-wise distribution of cost of credit of the sample borrowers in Maynaguri block.

Table 3.20 shows that the borrowers under agricultural labourer class have incurred the lowest average cost of borrowing of Rs. 322 which is equal to 3.51 of the loan amount. The borrowers under medium farmer categorys have spent the highest average cost of borrowing of Rs. 555 representing 1.39 percent of the average credit availed. The borrowing cost as percent of credit availed shows that no significant variations exist between small farmer (3.50 percent) and agricultural labourer (3.51 percent) category respectively.

Table 3.20: Farm Size-Wise Distribution of Cost of Credit in the Selected Villages under Maynaguri Block

Farm size	*No. of borrowers*	*Mean cost of credit (Rs.)*	*Mean credit supplied (Rs.)*	*Cost of borrowing as % of credit availed*
SF	22	450	12864	3.50
MF	16	425	13125	3.24
MF*	6	555	40000	1.39
AL	9	322	9167	3.51
Total	53	425	15387	2.76

Source: Field Survey, 2006-07.

Farm size-wise classification of cost of credit under Jalpaiguri sadar presented in Table 3.21 shows that borrowers under agricultural labourer class have incurred the lowest average cost of credit of Rs. 291 representing 2.86 percent of the average loan amount. Whereas that borrowers under medium farmer category have spent the highest average cost of credit of Rs. 560 which is equal to 1.6 percent of the average credit. The corresponding average cost of credit under small farmer and marginal farmer category are Rs. 331 and Rs. 351 respectively which are equal to 2.17 percent and 2.74 percent of the credit availed. The diagrammatic presentation of cost of borrowing credit is given in Figure 3.3.

Figure 3.3: Cost of Borrowing in Blocks

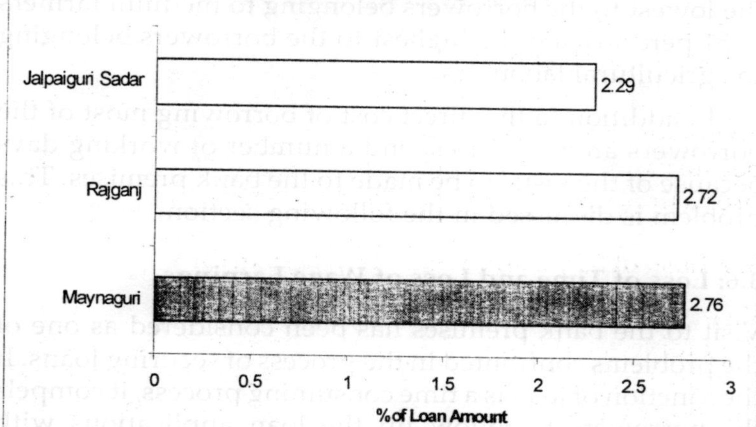

Table 3.21 : Farm Size-Wise Cost of Credit under Jalpaiguri Sadar

Farm size	*No. of borrowers*	*Mean cost of credit (Rs.)*	*Mean credit supplied (Rs.)*	*Cost of borrowing as % of credit availed*
SF	17	331	15265	2.17
MF	23	351	12826	2.74
MF*	6	560	35000	1.60
AL	8	291	10188	2.86
Total	54	359	15667	2.29

Source: Field Survey, 2006-07.

The above analysis reveals that borrowers are compelled to spend substantial amount to get the credit. The borrowers under Maynaguri block have incurred 2.76 percent of the loan amount as borrowing cost which is quite high by any standard. It is clear from the survey that inter-block variations in borrowing cost may be due to frequent visits to bank branches as a result of delay in selection and disbursement of the loans. Each visit involves opportunity cost for the farmers.

Farm size-wise analysis reveals that borrowing cost is the lowest to the borrowers belonging to medium farmers (1.51 percent) and the highest to the borrowers belonging to agricultural labourers.

In addition to the direct cost of borrowing most of the borrowers are forced to spend a number of working days because of the visits to be made to the bank premises. This problem is discussed in the following section.

3.6: Loss of Time and Loss of Wage Earnings

Visit to the bank premises has been considered as one of the problems confronted in the process of securing loans. If the sanction of loan is a time consuming process, it compels the borrowers to follow up the loan applications with frequent visits to the bank. This results in loss of time and ultimately in the loss of wage earnings. This loss of earnings actually increases the cost of obtaining the loan. This in turn reduces the actual amount of money available for the purpose for which the loan was sanctioned. This situation is worse particularly in the case of poor borrowers who have no other source of income[3].

Keeping this in view the borrowers in the present study have asked to state the number of visits paid by them between the filing of application and final disbursement of the loan. The experiences of the interviewed borrowers show that the borrowers had to visit the branches a good number of times even after filing the application. It can be observed from table 3.22 that the small and medium farmers require to visit twice, 30.77 percent of the marginal farmers and 29.17 percent of the agricultural labourers have visited the bank premises more than five times (each such visit involves opportunity cost for the farmers). While this may be partly due to the fact that marginal farmers and agricultural labourers are educationally backward[4], it is comment on the free flow of necessary information to the borrowers.

Table 3.22: Number of Visits to Bank Premises after Filling the Application

No. of Visits	*SF*	*MF*	*MF**	*AL*
2 times	64(100)	27	20(100)	12
3 times	-	9	-	5
More than 5 times	-	16(30.77)	-	7(29.17)
Total	64	52	20	24

Figures in the parentheses indicate percentages

Source: Interview Responses.

Now, on the basis of time taken for visiting the bank premises and the total number of visits, the loss of working days of each borrower has been estimated. A working day lost means 8 hours absence from work. Wage rate per day has been worked out in consultation with the sample borrowers, taking into consideration the wage rates prevailing in the study area. Loss of earnings of each borrower is estimated in above manner. The loss of wages as percentage of credit availed is calculated by using the following formula:

$$\frac{\text{Mean loss of wages}}{\text{Mean credit availed}} \text{ X } 100$$

The data obtained are shown in table 3.22 represent that on an average each borrower was absent 1.02 days from work for obtaining loan and the mean loss of wages was Rs. 76.84 which represents 0.47 percent of borrowed amount. The loss of working days, loss of earnings and loss of earnings as a percent of credit availed among the farm sizes are also in Table 3.22.

3.6.1 Farm Size-Wise Loss of Wage Earnings

Table 3.23 exhibits the farm size-wise mean loss of working days, loss of wages and percentage of loss of wages to the borrowed amount. Farm size-wise analysis discloses that the mean loss of working days is high in the case of borrowers belonging to marginal farmers (1.20 days) and lowest in the case of borrowers belonging to small farmers (0.88 days). The loss of wages of the borrowers belonging to small, marginal and medium farmers and agricultural labourers comes to 0.46, 0.63, 0.21 and 0.82 percent of the amount of credit availed by the borrowers. The diagrammatic presentation of loss of wage earnings is presented in figure 3.4.

Figure 3.4: Loss of Wage Earnings (Percentage of Loan Amount)

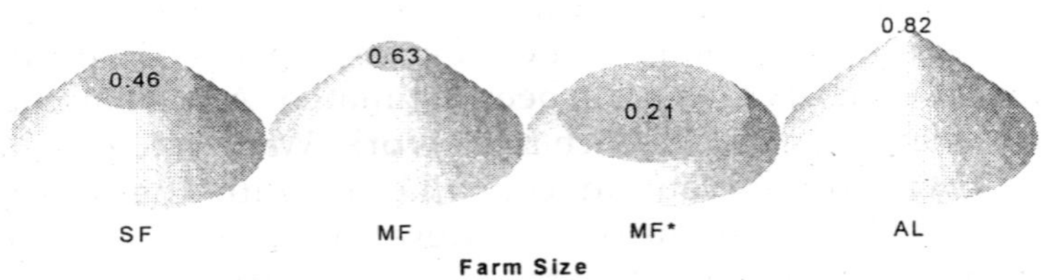

Table 3.23: Farm Size-Wise Classification of Mean Loss of Working Days and Loss of Earnings

Farm size	*No. of borrowers*	*Mean loss of working days*	*Mean loss of earnings (Rs.)*	*Loss of earnings as % of credit availed*
SF	64	0.88	66.00	0.46
MF	52	1.2	90.00	0.63
MF*	20	1.00	75.00	0.21
AL	24	1.05	78.75	0.82
Total	160	1.02	76.84	0.47

Source: Field Survey, 2006-07.

The above analysis indicates that the borrowers have spent a number of working days to visit the bank premises to obtain loan. On each visit they have spent time and money besides losing their wage earnings. The study reveals that on an average each borrower has spent 1.02 working days to get the loan. This has resulted in a loss of wages equivalent to Rs. 76.84, which may be due to delay in sanctioning the loan amounts, lack of information. From the study we also find that loss of wage earnings is the highest in the case of borrowers belonging marginal farmers and agricultural labourers in the district. Possibly due to lack of information the borrowers belonging to marginal farmers and agricultural labourers have visited the bank premises frequently and as such the loss of wages as a percentage of credit availed is the highest for those borrowers.

This chapter has analysed the socio-economic profile of the borrowers, credit needs of the farmers, the time lag in getting credit, cost of borrowings and loss of wage earnings. The socio-economic profile of borrowers reveals that of the respondents, 32.5 percent possess only less than one acre of land. About 68 percent of the sample borrowers have a family size of 3 to 5 members. Nearly 42 percent of the sample respondents have no formal education. 76.25 percent of the respondents are males and 48.75 percent of the respondents are in the age group of 15-40. The backward classes, scheduled castes and scheduled tribes constitute 90.62 percent of the sample.

The analysis on credit requirement indicates that the UBKGB has failed to meet the credit need of the borrowers. The UBKGB has supplied inadequate funds for the activities undertaken by the borrowers in the district of Jalpaiguri. From the field survey it is observed that the ratio of mean credit obtained to the demand for credit is 66.45 percent. Thus 33.55 percent of the credit requirements of the borrowers is met by the UBKGB. This inadequacy of fund has possibly compelled the borrowers to depend on the informal sources of credit. The percentage of such credit gap is the highest in Jalpaiguri sadar block (39.83 percent) and in Jalpaiguri sadar, the borrowers belonging to medium farmers are in worse position as 66.56 percent of the credit requirements of medium farmers are not met by the UBKGB. The percentage of credit gap is the lowest (22.53 percent) in Rajganj block where the borrowers belonging to small farmers are in a better position regarding credit requirements as the credit needs of these categories are left unfulfilled to the extent of 11.76 percent. Similarly the credit needs of the borrowers belonging to small farmers in Maynaguri block are left unfulfilled to the extent of 17.54 percent.

The study shows that the sanctioning of loan is a time-consuming process. It is found that on an average 8.85 days are required by the bank for granting loans to the borrowers. The delayed receipt of loan is high in Maynaguri block (7.6 days) and in Maynaguri block the borrowers belonging to marginal farmers are in a worse position as the delay in granting credit to these borrowers is as high as 9.66 days. In Jalpaiguri sadar as well as in Rajganj block the borrowers belonging to medium farmers and agricultural labourers are in a worse position as in the case of medium farmers the average time taken by the UBKGB is as high as 10 days and for agricultural labourers the average time taken is 15 days.

The analysis on cost of borrowing credit reveals that borrowers are compelled to spend a substantial amount (average of Rs. 426) to obtain the loan from the bank. In percentage terms this works out to 2.60 percent of the loan amount obtained. A farm size-wise comparison shows that the borrowers belonging to medium farmers had to incur 1.51 percent of the loan amount as borrowing cost. The cost of borrowing is the lowest (2.29 percent) in Jalpaiguri sadar followed by Rajganj block (2.72 percent) and Maynaguri block (2.76 percent) respectively.

The study indicates that besides the cost of borrowings, the borrowers have to spend a number working days for making visits to the bank premises to obtain the credit. From the study we find that small and medium farmers required to visit the bank premises twice while about 31 percent of the marginal farmers and 29 percent of the agricultural labourers had to visit the branches more than five times. Thus the poor farmers incur higher transaction costs in availing funds. Due to the visits to the branches the borrowers have to spend about 1.02 working days on an average to get the loan and this has resulted in a loss of wages equivalent to 0.47 percent of the credit availed by them. The loss of wages is the highest in the case of borrowers belonging to marginal farmers (0.63 percent) and agricultural labourers (0.82 percent) respectively.

NOTES AND REFERENCES

1. Benson Kunjukunju and S. Mohanan (2002), *Institutional Finance and Rural Development*, New Century Publications, New Delhi.
2. Madhura Swaminathan, "The Microcredit Alternative" ? *Economic and Political Weekly*, March 31, 2007
3. Benson Kunjukunju and S. Mohanan, *op.cit.*, p.131.
4. About fifty-eight percent of the marginal farmers and seventy-nine percent of the agricultural labourers are illiterate in our sample, while only 16 percent of the small farmers are so.

4

Farmers' Experience with Bank Loans

4.1 Introduction

The process of getting loans from the bank is not an easy task. The borrowers have to face numerous difficulties and spend time and money tc get the loans. On many occasions, a major problem faced by the poor in approaching banks is that of the attitudes and behaviour of bank staff. Many of the poor often complain about the kind of behavour they receive while interacting with the banks. They are not treated properly because of discriminatory attitudes towards the poor[1]. Few of them can master the confidence to approach the banks and secure loans from them. Scant regard for the poor makes the problem of approaching the banks for loan more complicated. Many rural people feel reluctant to approach the banks and do not have enough courage because of their lowly livelihood, their humble clothes and their educational level. Problems of attitudes and behaviour of the staff become a major obstacle in reaching the poor people and other socially deprived. An attempt is made in this chapter to examine the problems faced by the borrowers in getting bank credit. These problems are classified under two heads, viz. (a) problems associated with the bank, and (b) financial problems.

4.2: Problems Associated with the Bank

A borrower, who faces a large number of problems in obtaining loans may develop a retaliatory attitude towards the bank[2]. During field survey the borrowers were asked to state the problems which they faced in getting loans from the bank. The information is collected on the type of problems faced by the borrowers in getting loans from the bank. In our present study five major problems have been identified. These are :

- Lack of co-operation of bank staff.
- Time gap in sanctioning loan.
- Recommendation of panchayet pradhan.
- Discriminatory behaviour of bank staff.
- Complicated loan procedure.

To examine the relative importance of each of these problems, the borrowers selected were asked to rank these problems in order of priorities. First of all, ranks are given to each problem and then weights are assigned to each problem in descending order[3]. Weight of 5, 4, 3, 2 and 1 are assigned to these problems. Problems connected with the credit institution are analysed in relation to blocks and farm sizes.

Table 4.1 shows the borrowers ranking of importance of various problems. From table 4.1 it is found that the borrowers have attached maximum value to the recommendation of panchayat pradhan (32.57 percent of the total score) followed by delay in sanctioning loan from the bank (30.57 percent) and complicated loan procedure (20 percent). Lack of co-operation of bank staff has been given fourth ranking (9.43percent). Discriminatory behaviour of bank staff has been given least importance (7.43 percent).

Table 4.1: Borrowers' Ranking of Importance of Various Problems

SL. No.	Problems	Priorities					Total Score	%age to Total
		1st	2nd	3rd	4th	5th		
1.	Lack of Co-operation of Bank Staff	10	-	2	-	-	66	9.43
2.	Recommendation of Panchayat Pradhan	32	10	8	-	4	228	32.57
3.	Time Gap in Sanctioning Loan	36	7	-	-	6	214	30.57
4.	Complicated Loan Procedure	25	-	5	-	-	140	20
5.	Discriminatory Behaviour of Bank Staff	8	-	-	5	2	52	7.43
	Total						700	100

Source: Interview Responses

Borrowers' problems in getting loans from the bank are analysed block-wise and farm size-wise in each block in the forthcoming section.

4.2.1 Block-Wise Classification of Problems in Getting Credit

Block-wise classification of problems discloses that problems of borrowers in the process of obtaining loans vary from block to block (Table 4.2, 4.3 and 4.4).

From the table 4.2 it is clear that delay in sanctioning loan is the foremost problem faced by the borrowers in Maynaguri block because the borrowers have attached maximum value to the delay in sanctioning loan (31.36 percent to total score). The next important problem which the borrowers have faced in obtaining loan from the bank is the recommendation of panchayat pradhan. In this case the borrowers have assigned the maximum value (30.08 percent). Lack of co-operation of bank staff score the lowest (4.66 percent).

Table 4.2: Borrowers' Ranking of Importance of Various Problems in Maynaguri Block

SL. No.	*Problems*	*Priorities*					*Total*	*%age to*
		1st	*2nd*	*3rd*	*4th*	*5th*	*Score*	*Total*
1.	Lack of Co-operation of Bank staff	2	-	-	-	1	11	4.66
2.	Recommendation of Panchayat Pradhan	10	2	4	-	1	71	30.08
3.	Time Gap in Sanctioning Loan	14	1	-	-	-	74	31.36
4.	Complicated Loan Procedure	7	2	1	-	-	46	19.49
5.	Discriminatory Bevavour of Bank staff	4	2	2	-	-	34	14.41
	Total						236	100

Source: Interview Responses.

Table 4.3 presents the problem faced by the borrowers in Rajganj block. From the table it is found that delay in sanctioning of loan has emerged as the major problem of the respondents in Rajganj block. In this case the borrowers have assigned the highest score (40.65 percent). The second important problem of the borrowers is the recommendation of panchayet pradhan. Complicated loan procedure is ranked as the third problem by the borrowers (21.96 percent). Thus the borrowers in Rajganj block also have faced the same type of problems like Maynaguri block.

Table 4.3: Borrowers' Ranking of Importance of Various Problems in Rajganj Block

SL. No.	*Problems*	*Priorities*					*Total*	*%age to*
		1st	*2nd*	*3rd*	*4th*	*5th*	*Score*	*Total*
1.	Lack of Co-operation of Bank staff	1	-	-	-	4	9	4.21
2.	Recommendation of Panchayat Pradhan	10	2	-	-	-	58	27.10

3.	Time Gap in Sanctioning Loan	13	4	2	-	-	87	40.65
4.	Complicated loan procedure	5	4	2	-	-	47	21.96
5.	Discriminatory Behaviour of Bank Staff	1	1	-	-	4	13	6.07
	Total						214	100

Source: Interview Responses

The problems faced by the borrowers in Jalpaiguri sadar is presented in Table 4.4. From Table 4.4 it is found that recommendation of panchayt pradhan is ranked as the main problem because in this case the respondents have assigned the highest score (39.60 percent). The time lag in getting credit merges as the second important problem. In this case the percentage to total score is 21.20.

Table 4.4: Borrowers' Ranking of Importance of Various Problems in Jalpaiguri Sadar

SL. No.	*Problems*	*Priorities*					*Total*	*%age to*
		1st	*2nd*	*3rd*	*4th*	*5th*	*Score*	*Total*
1.	Lack of Co-operation of Bank staff	8	-	2	-	-	46	18.4
2.	Recommendation of Panchayat Pradhan	15	6	-	-	-	99	39.6
3.	Time Gap in Sanctioning Loan	7	3	2	-	-	53	21.2
4.	Complicated Loan Procedure	8	1	1	-	-	47	18.8
5.	Discriminatory Behaviour of Bank staff	1	-	-	-	-	5	2
	Total						250	100

Source: Interview Responses

Thus the major hurdles of borrowers in Jalpaiguri sader block are recommendation of local Panchayat Pradhan and time gap in sanctioning loans. Now to examine the similarity in the ranking of problems faced by the borrowers among different blocks correlation co-efficient has been used. For this purpose data presented in tables 4.2, 4.3 and 4.4 are arranged in Table 4.5.

Table 4.5: Block-wise Classification of Problems faced by the Borrowers

SL. No.	*Problems*	*Maynaguri*		*Rajganj*		*Jalpaiguri Sadar*		*Total*
		Total Score	*Rank*	*Total Score*	*Rank*	*Total Score*	*Rank*	
1.	Lack of Co-operation of Bank staff	11	5	9	5	46	4	66
2.	Recommendation of Panchayat Pradhan	71	2	58	2	99	1	228
3.	Time Gap in Sanctioning Loan	74	1	87	1	53	2	214
4.	Complicated Loan Precedure	46	3	47	3	47	3	140
5.	Discriminatory Behaviour of Bank staff	34	4	13	4	5	5	52

Source: Interview Responses Rank correlation coefficient : Maynaguri and Rajganj=1

Rajganj and Jalpaiguri= 0.80

Maynaguri and Jalpaiguri =0.80

The rank correlation co-efficient (R) between Maynaguri and Rajganj blocks is 1 whereas the rank correlation co-efficient between Rajganj and Jalpaiguri sadar blocks and between Maynaguri and Jalpaiguri sadar blocks are the same i.e., 0.80. Thus the correlation coefficient between three blocks are high which shows that the rankings are similar in three blocks.

4.3.2: Farm-Size-Wise Classification of Problems in Getting Credit

The relationship between farm size-wise classification and the problems connected with the bank faced by the respondents in obtaining loan is analysed here.

Let us first consider the problem faced by the borrowers under different farm-sizes in Maynaguri block.

Data presented in Table 4.6 represent farm size-wise classification of problems in obtaining loans from UBKGB in Maynaguri block. The problems highlighted in Table 4.6 reveals that time gap is the major constraint to the borrowers belonging to small farmers. Recommendation and discriminatory behaviour of bank staff are ranked second and third among the problems faced by small farmers. Recommendation by panchayet pradhan is considered as the major constraint to the borrowers belonging to marginal and medium farmers. It is found that delay in sanctioning credit is the foremost problem to the borrowers belonging to agricultural labourers. The correlation between small farmers and marginal farmers is only high(0.80) which shows that the rankings are similar between small and marginal farmers in Maynaguri block.

Table 4.6: Farm Size-wise Classification of Problems in Maynaguri Block

SL. No.	*Problems*	*Farm size*							
		SF		*MF*		*MF**		*AL*	
		Total Score	*Rank*	*Total Score*	*Rank*	*Total Score*	*Rank*	*Total Score*	*Rank*
1.	Lack of Co- operation of Bank staff	5	5	3	5	1	5	2	5
2.	Recommendation of Panchayat Pradhan	25	2	25	1	11	1	10	3
3.	Time Gap in Sanctioning Loan	30	1	23	2	3	4	18	1
4.	Complicated Loan Procedure	12	4	15	3	4	3	15	2
5.	Discriminatory Behaviour of Bank staff	19	3	5	4	5	2	5	4

Source: Interview Responses Rank correlation coefficient: SF and MF=.80, SF and MF*=.40, SF and AL=.70, MF* and MF=.60, MF* and AL=0.10, MF and AL=0.70.

Farm size-wise classification of problems connected with the bank in Rajganj block highlighted in table 4.7 reveals that complicated loan procedure is considered as the major constraint to the small farmers and delay in sanctioning credit is the next important problem to them. Time lag and recommendation are the major two important problems to marginal farmers and agricultural labourers. While the borrowers belonging to medium farmers find a reversal of the constraints indicated above. The correlation between the small and marginal farmers is low which shows that the rankings of problems are not similar between them. The correlation between the small and medium farmers is negative which represents the two sets of ranks are just the opposite. Since the rank correlation coefficient between the marginal farmers and agricultural labourers is the largest value, the rankings of problems are almost the same.

Table 4.7: Farm Size-wise Classification of Problems in Rajganj Block

SL. No.	Problems	*Farm size* SF Total Score	SF Rank	MF Total Score	MF Rank	MF* Total Score	MF* Rank	AL Total Score	AL Rank
1.	Lack of Co- operation of Bank staff	2	5	2	5	3	3	2	4
2.	Recommendation of Panchayat Pradhan	24	3	14	2	15	1	5	2
3.	Time Gap in Sanctioning Loan	29	2	24	1	10	2	24	1
4.	Complicated Loan Procedure	39	1	4	4	1	5	3	3
5.	Discriminatory Behaviour of Bank staff	3	4	7	3	2	4	1	5

Source: Interview Responses Rank correlation coefficient : SF and MF= 0.40

SF and MF*= -0.20, SF and AL= 0.60, MF and MF*= 0.60, MF* and AL= 0.60, MF and AL=0.70

Farm-size-wise classification of problems in getting credit from UBKGB in Jalpaiguri sader is presented in table 4.8

Table 4.8: Farm Size-wise Classification of Problems in Getting Loans in Jalpaiguri Sadar

SL. No.	Problems	*Farm size* SF		MF		MF*		AL	
		Total Score	*Rank*	*Total Score*	*Rank*	*Total Score*	*Rank*	*Total Score*	*Rank*
1.	Lack of Co- operation of Bank staff	11	3	25	3	5	2	5	3
2.	Recommendation of Panchayat Pradhan	38	1	36	1	10	1	15	1
3.	Time Gap in Sanctioning Loan	8	4	31	2	4	3	10	2
4.	Complicated Loan Precedure	30	2	10	4	3	4	4	4
5.	Discriminatory Behaviour of Bank staff	1	5	2	5	1	5	1	5

Source: Interview Responses Rank correlation coefficient : SF and MF= 0.60 SF and MF* = 0.70, SF and AL = 0.60, MF and MF* = 0.90, MF and AL =1,MF* and AL= 0.90

Table 4.8 shows that recommendation of panchayat pradhan has emerged as the major problem faced of the borrowers belonging to small, marginal, medium and agricultural labourers respectively. Complicated loan procedure is ranked as second problem to the small farmers while delay in sanctioning loan has emerged as the second major constraint to marginal farmers and agricultural labourers. Lack of co-operation of bank staff is found as the second problem to the medium farmers. The rank correlation between marginal and medium farmers, between marginal and agricultural labourers and between medium farmers is0.90 and above, which shows that the rankings are almost same.

Now to examine the similarity in the rankings of problems faced by different farm sizes in three blocks (combined), data presented in tables 4.6, 4.7 and 4.8 are arranged in Table 4.9.

Table 4.9: Farm-Size Wise Classification of Problems Connected With Bank

Problems	*Farm size*							
	SF		*MF*		*MF**		*AL*	
	Weighted Score	*Rank*	*Weighted Score*	*Rank*	*Weighted Score*	*Rank*	*Weighted Score*	*Rank*
Lack of Co-operation Of Bank Staff	18	5	30	3	9	3	9	4
Recommendation of Prodhan	87	1	75	2	36	1	30	2
Time Lag in Getting Loan	67	3	78	1	17	2	52	1
Complicated Loan Procedure	81	2	29	4	8	4.5	22	3
Discriminatory Behaviour Of Bank Staff	23	4	14	5	8	4.5	7	5

Rank correlation coefficient : SF and MF= 0.30, SF and MF*= 0.43, SF and AL= 0.60, MF and MF*= 0.88, MF and AL= 0.90, MF*and AL= 0.72.

Source: Field Survey, 2006-07.

Table 4.9 shows that delay in sanctioning credit and recommendation of pradhan are found to be the major problems to the borrowers belonging to marginal farmers and agricultural labourers while the borrowers belonging to medium farmers find a reversal of these constraints. The recommendation of pradhan and complicated loan procedure are ranked as the major constraints to the small farmers. The correlation between medium farmers and agricultural labourers, between medium and marginal farmers and between marginal farmers and agricultural labourers is 72 and above which shows that the rankings of problems are similar between them.

4.4: Financial Problems Faced by Sample Borrowers in the Process of Obtaining Loans.

The farmers being the borrowers of banks, are asked details with respect to their impressions about bank financing in terms of factors such as inadequate amount of credit, high borrowing cost etc. The specific statements that have been canvassed for this purpose are:

- High borrowing cost of credit
- Loss of wages due to making a number of visits to bank premises in connection with borrowing of loan.
- Inadequate amount of credit.
- Demand for bribes.

Farmers' responses to these are recorded only after ensuring that each one of the queries is clearly understood by the respondents[4].

The analysis of the responses of the sample borrowers reveals that the cost of borrowing credit is too high and is ranked as the main problem. The second major problem faced in the process of loan taking is loss of wages due to frequent visits to the bank premises. Inadequate amount of credit is ranked as the third major problem. The various financial problems faced by the borrowers are indicated in the Tables 4.10 and 4.11.

Block-wise classification of financial problems presented in table 4.10 reveals that high borrowing cost is considered as the major constraint to the borrowers in Maynaguri block followed by the loss of wages. In Jalpaiguri and Rajganj blocks however the borrowers find a reversal of the constraints indicated above. The correlation coefficient between Maynaguri, Jalpaiguri and Rajganj blocks is high. This shows that rankings of problems are similar between these blocks.

Table 4.10: Block-Wise Classification of Financial Problems

Problems	Maynaguri block		Jalpaiguri block		Rajganj block		Total weighted score	Rank
	Weighted Score	Rank	Weighted score	Rank	Weighted score	Rank		
High borrowing cost	63	1	46	2	51	2	160	1
Loss of wages	47	2	55	1	52	1	154	2
Inadequate amount of credit	32	3	32	3	33	3	97	3
Demand for bribes	25	4	30	4	31	4	86	4

Rank correlation coefficient : Maynaguri and Jalpaiguri =0.80, Jalpaiguri and Rajganj = 1

Maynaguri and Rajganj = 0.80

Source: Interview Responses

Table 4.11: Farm-Size-Wise Classification of Financial Problem

Problems	SF		MF		MF*		AL	
	Weighted Score	Rank	Weighted Score	Rank	Weighted Score	Rank	Weighted Score	Rank
High Borrowing Cost	67	1	48	1	10	4	35	1.5
Loss of Wages	52	3	47	2	20	1	35	1.5
Inadequate Amount of Credit	55	2	21	4	13	3	8	4
Demand for Bribe	25	4	32	3	14	2	15	3

Rank correlation coefficient : SF and MF =0.40, SF and MF*= -0.60,

SF and AL= 0.25, MF and AL = 0.95, MF* and AL= 0.15

Source : Interview Responses

In connection with financial problems faced by borrowers of the study area in relation to different farm sizes (table 4.11), it is found that high borrowing cost is the foremost problem to the small farmers followed by inadequate amount of credit. High borrowing cost is ranked as the main problem to the borrowers belonging to marginal farmers followed by loss of alternative wages. While loss of wages has emerged as major constraint to the borrowers belonging to medium farmers. The borrowers belonging to agricultural labourers have assigned the same rank to the loss of wages and high borrowing cost. The correlation coefficient between marginal farmers and agricultural labourers is 0.95,which shows that the rankings of problems are similar.

4.5: Conclusion

On the basis of above analysis we find that the problems associated with the bank vary from block to block. Delay in sanctioning credit, recommendation of pradhan and complicated loan procedure are the primary problems faced the borrowers in Maynaguri, Jalpaiguri sadar and Rajganj blocks respectively. Recommendation of panchayat pradhan has emerged as the major problem to the borrowers belonging to small and marginal farmers while delay in sanctioning credit is ranked as main constraint to marginal farmers and agricultural labourers.

Of the various financial problems faced by the borrowers high borrowing cost is the main problem to the borrowers in Maynaguri block while loss of wage earnings is considered as the major problem to the borrowers in Jalpaiguri sadar and Rajganj blocks. Similarly high borrowing cost is ranked as the major constraint by the borrowers belonging to small farmers, marginal farmers and agricultural labourers respectively. The loss of wages is found as the major difficulty facing the medium farmers.

Thus to achieve the broader goals, the UBKGB has to put in considerable efforts to clear off farmers' doubt regarding the roles of the bank and also there exists a need for simplification of the lending procedures and flexibility of financial scale. The analysis of negative aspect of obtaining loans from UBKGB shows that the negative scene is characterized by many problems like delay in sanctioning credit, high borrowing cost, recommendation of pradhan etc. Hence for an effective result-oriented role of credit disbursed by the bank, it is necessary to remove the problems indicated above. In the next chapter, an attempt is made at analyzing the information regarding utilization of loans, repaying capacity of borrowers and repayment performance.

NOTES AND REFERENCES

1. Sunil Kumer (1990), Regional Rural Banks and Rural Development, Deep and Deep Publications, New Delhi.
2. Dr. Benson Kunjukunju and Dr. S. Mohanan (2002), Institutional Finance and Rural Development, New Century Publications, New Delhi.
3. The weight pattern is based on the priority given by the borrowers to the problems faced by them. The problem which gets the first priority will get the highest weight, i.e., equal to 5 (because there are five problems); similarly the second problem will get equal to 4, and so on.
4. In our sample forty-eight percent of the borrowers are illiterate and hence we have faced the greatest difficulty in eliciting replies to the questions in the schedules from the illiterate borrowers regarding the problems in obtaining loans from the bank.

5

Utilization of Loan, Repaying Capacity and Repayment Performance of Borrowers

5.1 Introduction

Credit is considered as one of the main inputs in any economic activity and such credit, if used properly, can create wealth for the upliftment of the weaker sections of the society. It is believed that utilisation of credit for a scheduled productive purpose has a direct bearing on the repayment behaviour of the borrowers. Productive utilization of borrowed money and timely repayment of due instalments largely determine the success of a lending institution. Repayment of loan in time is a main factor as it helps the bank to run its business. It also benefits the farmers by reducing their debt burden and helps them get a fresh loan in future[1]. while unproductive utilisation and irregular repayment or non-repayment of loan has certain depressing effects on the credit institutions as these dilute the entire loaning business. For example, if credit advanced for crop production is used for consumption or unproductive purposes, the resultant impact on agricultural productivity will be different from what was expected from proper use of it. Such diversion may adversely affect the repayment performance of the borrowers which in turn leads to overdues.

In this present chapter an attempt has been made to examine the extent of utilization of agricultural loan, repaying capacity and repayment performance of the borrowers. The reasons for default of loans in the study area are also analyzed. The chapter is divided into three sections. First section deals with utilization pattern of loans. Second section presents repaying capacity and repayment performance of the borrowers and the last section examines the reasons for default of the borrowers.

5.2 Utilisation Pattern of Loans

It is generally believed that credit should be used for the required purpose for which it has been sanctioned. Productive utilization borrowed money coupled with timely repayment of loans largely determines the success of a lending institution[2]. The usefulness of credit is determined by the extent of benefit of the farmers and the proper utilization of credit enables to raise agricultural productivity. But the difficulty arises when the credit given for the particular purposes are misutilised. It becomes the burden on the borrowers and creates the problem of overdues.

In view of the importance of the proper utilisation of loan for a scheduled productive purpose, a direct interview of the borrowers was conducted to get information regarding utilisation of loans by sample borrowers. But in collecting data we faced the greatest difficulty in eliciting replies to the questions in the schedules from the reluctant and illiterate farmers. Even after much effort we got success in knowing the responses of the sample borrowers regarding uses of credit. The utilization of agricultural credit for the allotted purpose is presented in table 5.1. The table indicates that 143 borrowers out of 160 (89.38 percent) utilized the loan for the required purposes and 10.62 percent of them did not utilise the loan for the scheduled productive purposes. During field survey some borrowers have reported that they have used the loan to meet their social needs and immediate medical requirements partly due to poverty and partly due to ignorance.

Table 5.1: Utilisation of Agricultural Credit for the Required Purposes

No. of responding borrowers	*No. of borrowers who utilised the loan for the required purpose*	*No. of borrowers who did not utilise the loan for the required purpose*
160	143	17
Percentage	89.38	10.62

Source: Interview Responses.

5.2.1: Extent of Diversion of Credit

Utilisation of credit is normally examined in the context of the purpose for which the loan has been advanced and the purpose for which it has been actually used. The difference between the two represents the extent of diversion of credit. Diversion of credit from productive activities to unproductive activities creates a challenge for all people as it reduces the benefit of the borrowers. The problem of diversion of credit in the district was affecting the repaying capacity of the borrowers adversely and leading to defaults.

During field survey the borrowers were asked to state the purposes for which they availed the loan.It was found that the borrowers availed crop loans and business loans. In this present study the utilisation level is classified into three heads, viz.,

utilised in full,

utilised in part,

and not utilised at all.

The utilization pattern of crop loans by the sample borrowers is presented in table 5.2. The table 5.2 reveals that 66.94 present of the borrowers (81 out of 121 responding borrowers) have fully utilized the crop loan for the intended purposes, whereas 23.14 percent have partially utilized it for the required purpose and 7.44 percent of the borrowers did not properly utilize the loan availed. Thus overall 33.06 percent of the borrowers have misused the loan availed. It means that they have spent a part of the loan for the required purpose and another part of the loan for the unproductive purpose. This highlights the acute problem of the diversion of crop loan in the district of Jalpaiguri.

Table 5.2 : Extent of Utilisation of Crop Loan in the District

		No. of Borrowers			
Farm size	*Total*	*Utilized in Full*	*Utilized in part*	*Not utilized at all*	*Total misutilised*
SF	59	44(74.58)	13(22.05)	2(3.39)	15(25.42)
MF	42	26(61.90)	10(23.81)	6(14.29)	16(38.10)
MF*	20	11(55)	5(25)	4(20)	9(45)
AL	-	-	-	-	-

MF* indicates medium farmers

Source: Field Survey, 2006-07.

The study further shows that 74.58 percent of the borrowers under small farmers category have fully utilised the loan for the required purpose whereas 25.42 preen have misused the loan advanced for crop activities. 61.90 percent of he borrowers under marginal farmers category have fully utilised the crop loan and about 38 percent have misutilised the credit advanced for crop production. While 55 percent of the borrowers under medium farmers category have fully utilised the credit for the intended purposes and 45 percent of them have not properly utilise the loan availed. The extent of misutilisation of crop loan by the borrowers is depicted in diagram 5.1.

Figure 5.1: Misutilization of Crop Loan by Borrowers

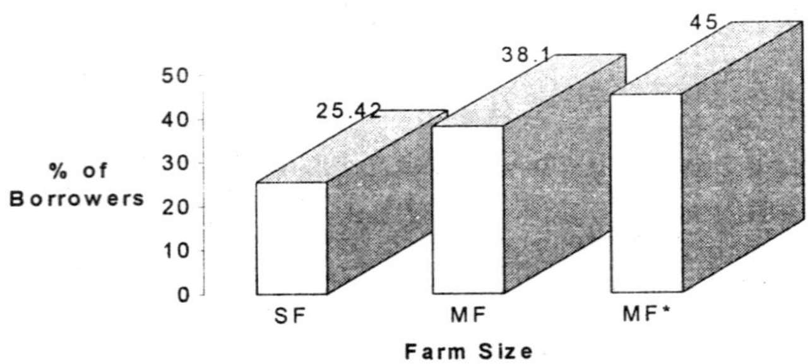

Table 5.3: Classification of Diverted Crop Loan in the District

	Borrowers who have partially spent the loan for the required purpose	
Percentage	*No*	*Percentage*
1-25	4	14.29
25-50	10	35.71
50-75	5	17.86
75-100	9	32.14
Total	28	100

Source: Opinion Survey

On the basis of the analysis of table 5.3, it is clear that 14.29 percent of the borrowers have utilised 1 to 25 percent of the loan for the required purpose. Similarly 35.71 percent of the borrowers have utilised 25 to 50 percent of loan, 17.86 percent of the borrowers have utilised 50 to 75 percent of the loan and 32.14 percent of the borrowers have spent the maximum i.e., 75 to 100 percent of loan for the required purpose. It is, therefore, clear that 50 percent of the borrowers have utilised less than 50 percent of the loan for the required purposes, spending remaining loan for unproductive purpose.

The utilization pattern of business loans availed by the borrowers is discussed with the help of Table 5.4.

Table 5.4: Extent of Utilisation of Business Loan*

	No.of Borrowers				
Farm size	*Total*	*Fully utilized*	*Partially utilized*	*Not utilized*	*Total misused*
SF	5	3(60)	1(20)	1(20)	2(40)
MF	10(100)	5(50)	4(40)	1(10)	5(50)
MF*	-	-	-	-	-
AL	24(100)	17(70.83)	4(16.67)	3(12.5)	7(29.17)
Total	39(100)	25(64.10)	9(23.07)	5(12.82)	14(35.90)

Source: Field Survey, 2006-07

* Also includes cattle loans

The Table 5.4 reveals that 64.10 percent of the borrowers (25 out of 39 responding borrowers) have fully utilised business loan whereas 23.07 percent have partially utilized the loan for the intended purposes and about 36 percent have not properly utilize the loan availed. It may be furthei noted that (table 5.4) 50 percent of the borrowers under marginal farmers category have misutilised the loan, while the corresponding percentages of borrowers under small farmers and agricultural laborer classes are 40 and 29.17 percent respectively. The extent of diverted business loan is shown in diagram 5.2.

Figure 5.2: Misutilization of Business Loan by Borrowers

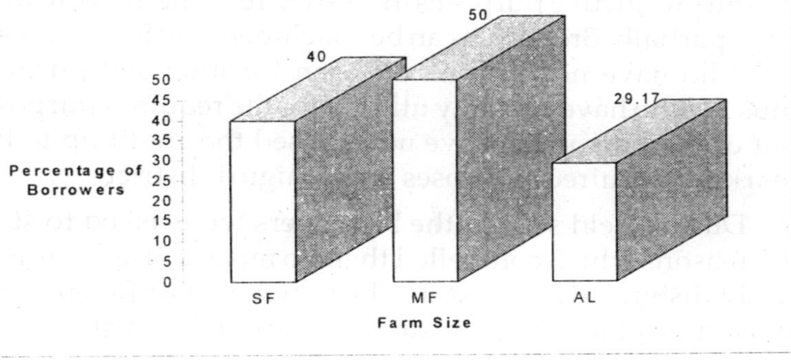

On the basis of the analysis of table 5.5, it is clear that 44.44 percent of borrowers have utilised 1 to 25 percent of cattle loan for the allotted purpose, similarly 44.44 percent of borrowers have utilised 25 to 75 percent of loan and remaining 11.12 percent of borrowers have spent 75 to 100 percent of loan availed. It is thus clear from the table 5.5 that 66.66 percent of borrowers have utilised less than 50 percent of loan for the required purpose.

Table 5.5 : Classification of Diverted Business Loan in the District

Borrowers who have partially utilised the loan for the required purpose		
Percentage of Loan	*No*	*Percentage*
1-25	4	44.44
25-50	2	22.22
50-75	2	22.22
75-100	1	11.12
Total	9	100

Source: Field Survey, 2006-07.

5.2.2 Causes of Diversion and Misuse of Agricultural Credit in the District

As we have stated earlier in this chapter that 17 borrowers out of 160 surveyed have not utilized the loan for the required purpose. It clearly indicates that they have diverted it from productive purposes to elsewhere while 37 borrowers have partially Broadly, it can be concluded that 54 borrowers (17 who have not utilised the loan for intended purpose plus 37 who have partially utilised for the required purpose) out of 160 borrowers have not utilised the credit up to the mark for required purposes in Jalpaiguri district.

During field survey the borrowers were asked to state the reasons which compelled them to misuse of agricultural credit disbursed by UBKGB. The flowing identified reasons are responsible for the misuse of credit in the district:

a. Inadequate amount of loan,
b. Illiteracy and ignorance,
c. Untimely credit,
d. Poverty
e. Spent on illness
f. Lack of proper Supervision.

Due to limited sources of income of borrowers, they are forced to divert the credit availed for members. It is fair to mention that the credit given to the borrowers in certain cases is found to be inadequate and this inadequacy is a cause for misuse of credit. During the visits to the borrowers for collection of data, some borrowers have reported that due to their illiteracy and ignorance they can not pull-up their credit financed activity properly and efficiently. It results in misuse of the loan. Some have borrowers reported that they can not get credit when they are in need because there is there is considerable time lag between the date of application for loan and date of sanctioning the loan. In the mean time they are forced to borrow money from local baniyas[3]. Due to acute poverty a large number of borrowers have misutilised the loan availed.

It is generally believed that institutional credit is designated as "supervised credit"[4]. The credit agencies have to play a more dynamic role by stressing the supervision and guidance aspects of credit more than credit deployment. But unfortunately these aspects have not yet received due recognition in the present institutional set up. Due to inadequate number of supervisory staff, they do not devote adequate time for supervision and guidance. On account of this, there is misutilisation of credit even when it is given for productive purposes.

On the basis of Table 5.6 the reasons responsible for the diversion and misuse of agricultural credit in Jalpaiguri district, the following meaningful conclusions may be derived.

It can be seen from table 5.6 that 25.93 percent of the borrowers who have misutilised the credit have reported that inadequacy of credit is the reason compelling them to do so. Diversion of loan amounts for lack of proper supervision is the second important reason for misuse as admitted by 18.52 percent of the borrowers. 16.67 percent of borrowers (9 out of 54) have reported that they can not get loan in time. The basic reason of delay in getting the loan is the lengthy formalities. That is why they can not use credit properly. 14.82 percent of the borrowers have misused the loan due to their acute poverty. Actually it seems relevant as 81.25 percent of the borrowers (130 out of 160) belong to small, marginal and landless categories in the district and only 18.75 percent are comparatively better off farmers. 12.96 percent of the borrowers have reported that the general illness of their family members is responsible for the misuse of credit on their part. 11.11 percent of the borrowers have disclosed that due to their illiteracy and ignorance they can not pull up the credit financed active properly and efficiently, which in turn have resulted in misuse of loan.

Table 5.6: Reasons of Diversion and Misuse of Credit

Reasons responsible for diversion and misuse of the credit	*No. of Misusing Borrowers*	*Percentage to total*
a) Inadequate amount of loan	14	25.93
b) illiteracy and ignorance	6	11.11
c) untimely credit	9	16.67
d) poverty	8	14.82
e) Spent on illness	7	12.96
f) lack of proper supervision	10	18.52
Total	54	100

Source: Field Survey, 2006-07

The foregoing analysis on utilisation of loans reveals that 33.75 percent of the borrowers (54 out of 160) have misutilised the loan either partially or fully. The study further shows that 33.06 percent of the borrowers have misused the crop loan and 35.90 percent borrowers have misused the business loan. Thus the incidence of misuse of loan by borrowers is comparatively high on business loan as compared to crop loan. In the district, diversion of credit for inadequacy of loan and lack of proper supervision are the two main reasons for misuse stated by the borrowers of crop and business activities. Since only a minority of borrowers misutilised the credit disbursed by UBKGB, the hypothesis that "majority of the borrowers misutilised the credit disbursed by UBKGB" is rejected here.

5.3 Repaying Capacity and Repayment Performance of the Sample Borrowers

Repayment of loan is a function both of repaying capacity and willingness to pay[5]. We first analyze in this section the repaying capacity of the borrowers of the study area. When credit is supplied by any agency, a major consideration is the repaying capacity of the person getting loan. It may be assumed that repayment performance will be good if the activities undertaken happen to generate sufficient income. The generation of income in fact shows the repaying capacity. Although the fact that repaying capacity and repayment performance may very, they may be taken positively associated in general.

The repaying capacity depends upon the returns from the activity or business in which the debtor is engaged. As repaying capacity depends on returns from the activity it is measured in our study in terms of surplus income from the activity. For this purpose during field survey the borrowers were asked to state whether they achieved have surplus income or not from the activity undertaken. Based on the information so collected an effort has been made in this section to find out the position of income generated from loans disbursed by the UBKGB. Table 5.7 and 5.8 discuss the income position generated from the activities against which the loan was sanctioned.

Since the repaying capacity is positively related to the viability of the activity against which the loan is sanctioned, we have shown position of income generated from the activity undertaken. The position of income generation from the activities i.e., from business and crop loans is analysed in Tables 5.6 and 5.7. 121 borrowers have obtained crop loan from the UBKGB. Out of 121 borrowers 43.80 percent of them have obtained surplus income and 32.23 percent of the borrowers are in deficit. 23.97 percent of them have responded that they have neither achieved any surplus nor accrued any deficit. From crop loan 35.59 percent of the borrowers under small farmers category have achieved surplus, 40.48 percent of marginal farmers and, 75 percent of medium farmers categories are in surplus. 47.46 percent of small farmers and 26.19 percent of marginal farmers have obtained deficit income from the utilisation of loans and 16.95 percent of small farmers, 33.33 percent of marginal farmers and 25 percent of medium farmers have obtained neither a surplus nor a deficit. In all, the loans granted for crop activities seem to be beneficial for those who have comparatively strong land-base (medium farmers). This requires a case for more equal distribution of land asset among the farmers. Table 5.7 shows the position of income generated from business activity for which UBKGB has provided loans to sample borrowers.

Table 5.7: Position of Income Generated from Crop Loan

Farm size	*Surplus*	*Deficit*	*Nil*	*Total*
SF	21(35.59)	28(47.46)	10(16.95)	59(100)
MF	17(40.48)	11(26.19)	14(33.33)	42(100)
MF*	15(75)	-	5(25)	20(100)
AL	-	-	-	-
Total	53(43.80)	39(32.23)	29(23.97)	121(100)

Source: Interview responses.

Table 5.8 : Position of Income Generated from Loans for Business

Farm size	*Surplus*	*Deficit*	*Nil*	*Total*
SF	4(80)	-	1(20)	5(100)
MF	3(30)	5(50)	2(20)	10(100)
MF*	-	-	-	-
AL	9(37.5)	9(37.5)	6(25)	24(100)
Total	16(41.02)	14(35.90)	9(23.08)	39(100)

Source: Interview responses

In all 39 borrowers were provided loans for business, 12.82 percent of small farmers, 25.64 percent of marginal farmers and 61.54 percent of landless labourer categories of the borrowers were provided loans for business purposes out of 100 percent of marginal farmers category of borrowers, 30 percent of them have responded that they have obtained a surplus income from utilization of loan and 50 percent of them have obtained deficit while 20 percent have responded that they have not achieved any surplus nor accrued any deficit. Out of 5 small farmers, 80 percent have responded that they have achieved a surplus income and the remaining 20 percent have responded that they have neither achieved a surplus nor a deficit from the utilisation of loan. While in the case of landless labourers, 37.5 percent of the borrowers have obtained surplus or deficit while 25 percent have neither achieved a surplus nor a deficit. Overall a majority of the borrowers (41.02 percent) who have received loans on business have responded that they have obtained a surplus from the activity, while 35.90 percent are in deficit and remaining 23.08 percent are neither in surplus nor in deficit. Thus we see that small farmers have been benefited most from the loans on business. Agricultural labourers also seem to have benefited from loans on business.This may be on account of the fact that in the absence of land they have to depend on business for their livelihood.On the other hand, medium farmers have not benefited from business activity. They are more interested in strengthening of their farm-base by taking loans for agricultural purposes.

5.3.1 Repayment Performance of the Sample Borrowers

The success, the viability and sustainability to be precise, of financing different activities of the rural poor does not depend only on the provision of financial assistance. It equally depends on the borrowers' capacity to repay their loans regularly so as to enable the banks to further recycle of funds. The credit cycle has three major segments: The first is to mobilize resources, the second to lend them to credit worthy borrowers and third to recover whatever has been lent so that the recovered amount may be recycled[6]. Recycling of fund is, therefore, an important determinant of credit expansion. This recycling of funds is seriously threatened by the tendency of the borrowers not to repay the loans. This tendency also results in increasing overdue accumulation year after year. Locking up of funds in overdue restricts the capacity to recycle and push up the loaning business of the banks. Hence the loan repayment with interest by borrowers is necessary for the smooth functioning of institutional credit system.

Based on the data so collected an effort has been made to find out the repayment habits of the loaness. The repayment performance of the borrowers have been analyzed in tables 5.9 and 5.10.

Table 5.9 shows the repayment performance of the sample borrowers who were given loans for crop production. Overall 30.58 percent of the borrowers have fully repaid the loan at the due date. 51.24 percent of the borrowers have partially repaid the loan. 18.18 percent of them have not paidback any single instalment. Table 5.9 further shows that 75 percent of the borrowers under medium farmers categories have not repaid a single installment. 33.90 percent of the borrowers under small farmer categories have repaid in full at the due date and 66.10 percent have repaid the loan amount in part. Under marginal farmer categories

28.57 percent of them have repaid in full while 54.76 percent of the borrowers have repaid the debt in part and 16.67 percent have not repaid a single instalment.Here fully repaid at due date is noticed in the case of small farmers (33.90 percent) and marginal farmers (28.57 percent) and medium farmers (25 percent) respectively. However, in terms of these types of loans also, 51.24 percent of borrowers are found to be making partially repayments.

Table 5.9: Repayment Performance of the Sample Borrowers for Crop Loans

	Repayment Level			
Farm size	*Fully Repaid at due date*	*Partially Repaid til date of survey*	*Nothing Repaid til date of survey*	*Total*
SF	20(33.90)	39(66.10)	-	59(100)
MF	12(28.57)	23(54.76)	7(16.67)	42(100)
MF*	5(25)	-	15(75)	20(100)
AL	-	-	-	-
Total	37(30.58)	62(51.24)	22(18.18)	121(100)

Source: Field Survey 2006-07.

Table 5.9 shows the repayment performance of the borrowers who were given loans for business purposes. While 90 percent of marginal farmers who have obtained such loans from UBKGB, are found to be repaying the loan amount partially and remaining 10 percent do not pay back any installment whereas 60 percent of the small farmers have repaid loan amount in part and 45.83 percent of the agricultural labourer classes are partially repaying the loan amount. 40 percent of the small farmers have not repaid even a single instalment and 4 Agricultural labourers or 16.67 percent of agricultural laboures do not pay back any instalment. Out of 24 agricultural laboures 37.5 percent of them have repaid the loan in full. An interesting reading is that 37.5 percent of the agricultural laboures are found to be repaying business loans in full while no other farmers come under this category. 60 percent of small farmers and 90 percent of marginal farmers are found to be repaying the loans partially while 10 percent of marginal farmers, 16.67 percent of agricultural laborers and 40 percent of small are found to be making no repayment. On the whole 58.97 percent of the total borrowers who have taken business loan are found to be making partial repayments.

Table 5.10: Repayment Performance of the Sample Borrowers for Business Loans

	Repayment Level			
Farm size	*Fully Repaid at due date*	*Partially Repaid until date of survey*	*Nothing Repaid until date of Survey*	*Total*
SF	-	3(60)	2(40)	5
MF	-	9(90)	1(10)	10
MF*	-	-	-	-
AL	9(37.5)	11(45.83)	4(16.67)	24(100)
Total	9(23.08)	23(58.97)	7(17.95)	39(100)

Source: Field Survey 2006-07

Table 5.11 shows the overall repayment performance of the sample borrowers. Overall 28.75 percent of the sample borrowers had repaid the loan in full at the due date, 53.12 percent of the borrowers had paid back the loan in part til the date of survey and 18.12 percent of the borrowers did not pay back any single installment of the debt. Of all the small farmers categories 31.25 percent of borrowers had repaid the loan in full and 65.62 percent had partially repaid the debt.In marginal farmers category 12 borrowers or 23.08 percent of the borrowers were making repayments fully, 32 borrowers or 61.54 percent of the borrowers were making partial repayments and 8 borrowers or 15.38 percent did not pay any single installment. Under medium farmers category 5 borrowers or 25 percent had repaid the loan amount fully and 158 borrowers or 75 percent were making no payments at all. Finally under landless labourer classes, 9 borrowers or 37.5 percent were making repayment fully, 11 borrowers or 45.83 percent had repaid the loans in part and 4 borrowers or 16.67 percent had not paid back the loan amount. Thus from the field study in the district it is found that only 28.75 percent of the borrowers had fully repaid the loans.

Table 5.11: Overall Repayment Performance of the Sample Borrowers

	Level of Repayment			
Farm size	*Fully Repaid at due date*	*Partially Repaid til date of survey*	*Nothing Repaid til date of Survey*	*Total*
SF	20(31.25)	42(65.62)	2(3.12)	64(100)
MF	12(23.08)	32(61.54)	8(15.38)	52(100)
MF*	5(25)	-	15(75)	20(100)
AL	9(37.5)	11(45.83)	4(16.67)	24(100)
Total	46(28.75)	85(53.12)	29(18.12)	160(100)

Source: Field Survey 2006-07

5.3.2 Repayment Performance of Loan Amount by the Borrowers

During field survey the data on Principal and interest repaid were collected by Perusing the loan Pass book and with the help of discussions with the borrowers. In this way loans outstanding and loans repaid of each borrower was determined.

Now in order to find out the loan repaid as percentage of loan outstanding we have used the following formula:

$$\frac{\text{Average loan repaid X 100}}{\text{Average loan outstanding}}$$

Loans outstanding and loan repaid of each borrower include Principal and interest. Table 5.12 indicates that average amount of principal and interest demanded by the

UBKGB is estimated at Rs. 9416.12 whereas the mean amount of loan repaid by the borrowers comes to Rs. 3449.01. Therefore loan repaid as percentage of loans outstanding is estimated as 36.63 percent. The repayment performance of the borrowers in the district according to farm-size is presented also in table 5.12. Farm-size wise analysis of loan repayment (table 5.12) reveals that in percentage terms, the repayment Performance is better for the medium farmers (48.85 percent) followed by marginal farmers (35.40 percent), agricultural labourers (29.94 percent) and small farmers (26.59 percent) respectively.

Activity-wise data contained in table 5.13 reveal that the repayment performance by the borrowers for business activity is lower that of crop activity. For crop activity the repayment performance is better than for the medium farmers (63.90 percent) and worse for the marginal farmers (53.86 percent) whereas the repayment performance for business activity is better for the agricultural labourers (57.60 percent) and worse for the marginal farmers (35.40 percent).The diagrammatic presentation of loan repaid position of the borrowers is given in Figure5.3.

Figure 5.3: Loan Repayment Position of Borrowers

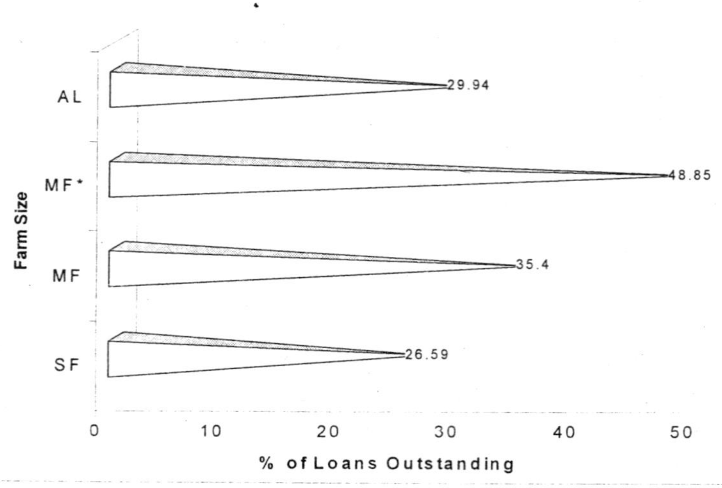

Table 5.12: Repayment Performance of Loans by the Borrowers in the District

Farm size	*Mean outstanding Loan (Rs)*	*Mean Loans Repaid*	*Loans Repaid as percent of Loans outstanding*
SF	2899.88	771.08	26.59
MF	2950.75	1044.50	35.40
MF*	2993.44	1462.19	48.85
AL	572.06	171.25	29.94
Total	9416.12	3449.01	36.63

Source: Field Survey, 2006-07

Table 5.13: Activity-wise Repayment Performance of Loans by the Borrowers

	Crop Activity		*Loan repaid*	*Business activity*		*Loan repaid*
	Mean outstanding loan	*Mean loan repaid*	*as %age of loan outstanding*	*Mean outstanding loan*	*Mean loan repaid*	*as %age of loan outstanding*
SF	11545	6374.97	55.22	1545	4429.8	38.37
MF	11803	6356.57	53.86	11803	4178	35.40
MF*	33932	21682	63.90	-	-	-
AL	-	-	-	6302	3629.92	57.60
Total	15334.88	8898.66	58.03	8384.69	3873	46.19

Source: Field Survey, 2006-07

It may be argued that the borrowers under medium farmers categories have the capacity to repay the loans regularly since 75 percent of the medium farmers has achieved surplus income obtained from the utilization of loan but they seem to be willful defaulters in repayment of loans as none of the medium farmers has repaid the loan amount in full (table 5.11). In the study it was also found that the most viable activity on which the UBKGB had sanctioned loan was crop production. Since 43.80 percent of the Sample borrowers who had received loans for such purposes the repayments habits showed that only 9 landless labourers or 23.08 percent of the borrowers do not have any overdue at the time of survey. This may be due to the fact that these loans are provided to small, marginal and agricultural labourers whose deficit income is more than surplus income what they have received for crop and business purposes. Thus they are not in a position to repay such loans regularly although they are willing to repay the loans. Hence it may be concluded that as far as repayment habits are concerned, it has been found to be poor.

The description gives also an account of the repayment performance of loan amount of the sample beneficiaries. The study shows a recovery of 36.63 percent of outstanding loan in the district. Hence the hypothesis that "there is a high amount of loan repaid" is rejected. Thus there is need to ensure the repayment of loans in order that the resources may be recycled in different activities through UBKGB'S loan.

5.3.3 Socio-Economic Study of the Repayment Performance of Sample Borrowers

In order to study the relationship between the socio-economic factors and repayment performance of the beneficiaries who have received loan from the UBKGB in the study area, five socio-economic factors have been considered here.

5.3.3.1 Sex-wise Repayment Performance

The data presented in table 5.14 offer sex-wise classification of the sample borrowers and their repayment level.

Table 5.14: Sex-Wise Distribution of Sample Borrowers and Repayment Performance

Level of Repayment	*Male*	*Female*	*Total*
1. Repaid in full	38(27.74)	8(34.78)	46(28.75)
2. Repaid in part	81(59.12)	4(17.39)	85(53.12)
3. Not Repaid at all	18(13.14)	11(47.83)	29(18.13)
Total	137(100)	23(100)	160(100)

Source: Field Survey, 2006-07 $\chi^2 = 24.73$; df=2, critical value at 5% level 5.99

The Table 5.14 shows that of the total size of 160 sample borrowers, 28.75 percent has repaid in full, 53.12 percent has repaid in part and remaining 18.12 percent of the borrowers have not repaid the loan at all. The table further shows that 34.78 percent of the female beneficiaries have repaid the full amount while in the case of males, the percentage of the male beneficiaries is more than the female beneficiaries. Under the category of not at all repaid, the percentage of female borrowers is more than the male borrowers.

In order to test the null hypothesis that there is no association between sex and repayment performance, Chi-square test has been applied. Since the calculated value (24.73) is greater than the table value (5.99) the null hypothesis is rejected and it has been concluded that there is a relationship between sex and repayment performance of the borrowers.

5.3.3.2 Age and Repayment Performance

Age and repayment performance of the borrowers are shown in table 5.15. It can be inferred from the table 5.15 that out of 160 borrowers in the age group up to 40 years, 29.59 percent of the borrowers have paid in full, 48.98 percent of them have paid in part and the remaining 21.43 percent do not pay at all. In the case of age-group above 40 years, improvement in percentages of partly paid is noticed but it is less under not at all and fully paid groups as compared to the age-group up to 40 years. The percentages are 29.27, 59.76 and 10.98 in the case of paid in full, party paid and not at all paid respectively.

The chi-square (χ^2) test shows that calculated value (2.402) < table value (5.99), the null hypothesis is accepted here. Therefore it can be concluded that age and repayment performance are not associated.

5.3.3.3 Social Group and Repayment Performance

In order to analyze the relationship between repayment performance and social group of the sample borrowers, social group has been classified into scheduled caste (SC),

Scheduled Tribe (ST) and Forward caste (FC). Table 5.16 shows the social groups and repayment performance of the sample borrowers.

Table 5.15: Age-Wise Classification of Repayment Performance

	Age Group (in years)		
Level of Repayment	*Up to 40*	*Above 40*	*Total*
1. Repaid in full	29(29.59)	17(27.42)	46(28.75)
2. Repaid in Part	48(48.98)	37(59.68)	85(53.12)
3. Not Repaid at all	21(21.43)	8(12.90)	29(18.13)
Total	98(100)	62(100)	160(100)

Source: Field Survey, 2006-07 χ^2= 4.50; df=2; critical value at 5% level 5.99

It can be inferred from the table 5.16 that in the case of ST, partly repaid is high in percentage compared to other Social groups i.e. SC and FC whereas the percentage of repaid in full is higher of the beneficiaries belonging to SC than the borrowers belonging to ST and FC. The percentages of not at all repaid are 17.39, 6.06 and 41.67 for SC, ST and FC respectively.

In order to test the relationship between caste and repayment habit, chi-square test has been formulated.

Table 5.16: Caste-wise Classification of Repayment Performance

Level of Repayment	*Scheduled Caste (SC)*	*Scheduled Tribe(ST)*	*Forward Cast(FC)*	*Total*
1.Repaid in full	23(36.51)	4(24)	17(23.61)	46(28.75)
2.Repaid in Part	30(47.62)	15(60)	40(55.56)	85(53.12)
3.Not Repaid at all	10(15.87)	4(16)	15(20.83)	29(18.13)
Total	63(100)	23(100)	74(100)	160(100)

Source: Sample Survey, 2006-07.

To test the null hypothesis that is, social group of the

borrowers is no influence in the repayment of loan, chi-square test has been applied. Here χ^2= 4.21 with df=4, now χ^2 0.05, 4= 9.488 (table value) since the calculated value is less than table value, the null hypothesis is accepted. Thus it can be concluded that caste of the borrowers has not influenced the repayment of loan.

Table 5.17: Education Level Wise Classification of Repayment of Loans

	Literacy Level			
Level of Repayment	*Illiterate*	*Primary*	*Secondary & Above*	*Total*
1.Repaid in full	8(11.94)	32(50.79)	6(20)	46(28.75)
2.Repaid in Part	47(70.15)	24(38.09)	14(46.67)	85(53.12)
3.Not Repaid at all	12(17.91)	7(11.11)	10(33.33)	29(18.13)
Total	67(100)	63(100)	30(100)	160(100)

Source: Sample Survey, 2006-07.

5.3.3.4 Education Level and Repayment Performance

It is believed that an educated person can make better use of credit and thus generate a surplus enough to repay the loan. Table 5.17 presents information on the education levels and repayment performance of the sample borrowers.

It is observed from the table that the repayment performance is better in the case of borrowers whose literacy level is up to primary level. In the case of beneficiaries who have no formal education, the percentage of partly repayment of loan is high (70.15 percent) whereas in the case of beneficiaries whose education level is up to primary level, the percentage of partly repayment of loan is low (38.09 percent). But under the category of not at all repaid, the percentage of borrowers whose education level is up to secondary above is more than the borrowers who have no formal education.

In order to test the relationship between literacy level and repayment performance, χ^2 test has been adopted. Here the calculated value (29.43) is greater than the table value (9.488) at 4 degree of freedom. Hence the hypothesis is rejected. Therefore, it can be concluded that literacy level has influenced the repayment performance of the borrowers.

5.3.3.5 Occupation and Repayment Performance

The repayment performance of the borrowers on occupation is presented in Table 5.18.

Table5.18: Occupation-Wise Repayment Performance

	Occupation		
Level of Repayment	*Borrowers who mainly depend on cultivation*	*Borrowers who do no depend on cultivation*	*Total*
1.Repaid in full	30(24.79)	16(41.03)	46(28.75)
2. Repaid in part	68(56.20)	17(43.59)	85(53.12)
3.Not Repaid at all	23(19.00)	6(15.38)	29(18.13)
Total	121(100)	39(100)	160(100)

Source: Sample Survey 2006-07.

It can be understood from the table 5.18 that repaid in full is higher in percentages in the case of beneficiaries who do not depend mainly on agriculture compared to those borrowers who depend on cultivation.The percentages of repaid in full are 24.79 and 41.03 for the borrowers who depend on cultivation and the borrowers who depend on other occupation respectively and repaid in part is high in the case of borrowers who depend on cultivation (56.20 percent) compared to borrowers who mainly depend on other occupation (43.59 percent) similarly not repaid at all are more for the borrowers who depend on cultivation (19.00).

Now in order to find out the relationship between repayment performance and occupation χ^2 test has been applied. Here the calculated value (3.79) is less than the table value (5.99). Hence the hypothesis is accepted. Therefore, occupation and repayment performance are independent.

5.3.4 Sources for Repayment

Prompt and regular repayment of loan is indispensable

for the expansion of rural credit. Repayment of any loan with having sufficient income is a problem-riden task for the poor borrowers. It my have an adverse implication of their being debt trapped.In this study it is important to know whether the borrowers are repaying the credit from the income accruing from the loan. For this purpose during field survey borrowers were asked to state the sources which were used to repay the loans.With the help of information collected through interviews an effort has been made to analyze the monetary sources of repayment.The situation in Jalpaiguri district in this respect may be shown with the help of the Table 5.19. The greatest difficulty in this study is in eliciting replies to the questions in schedules from the illiterate farmers. Even after much effort we have got success in knowing the response of cent percent borrowers regarding sources of repayment of loan.

Table 5.19: Income Earned from Credit Finance Activity and Refund of the Loan

No. of borrowers who have participated	*No. of borrowers who have repaid the loan from the income earned from credit financed activity*	*No. of borrowers who do not pay the debt from the income earned from credit financed activity*	*No. of borrowers who do not expect to repay the loan from the income likely to be earned from credit financed activity*
160	22	24	114
percentage	13.75	15	71.75

Source: Field Survey, 2006-07

Table 5.19 shows that 13.75 percent have refunded the loan from the additional income earned from proper utilization of credit for the intended purpose. 24 borrowers out of 160 (15 percent) have refunded the loan from other sources because they could not get sufficient income from the credit financed activity.71.75 percent were not hopeful of repaying the loan from the income likely to be earned from the credit financed activity. It represents that they have either misused the loan or circumstances have forced them to do so or the scheme was misconceived.

Table 5.20 shows that 24 borrowers out of 160 respondents have refunded the loan from sources other than the income earned from the credit financed activity, 66.67 percent of the sample respondents have taken loans from new type of gramin baniyas (mostly school teachers) with a promise to the lenders that the borrowers will return the amount (usually with higher interest) after receiving the fresh loan from the bank. Thus the borrowers begin a new gramin loan with a deficit on the capital. This leads to the creation of "debt cycles" for the borrowers. It is also important to note that 20.83 percent have managed to raise loans from Jalpaiguri People's Co-operative Bank and other banks for the repayment of loan installments and 3 borrowers (12.5 percent) have repaid the debt from other sources like Son's money order and income from secondary occupation.

Table 5.20: Sources of Refund other than the income from the Activity

	Other Sources			
No. of Borrowers who have participated	*No. of borrowers who have responded*	*Raising Loans from New Types of Baniyas*	*Raising Loans from other institutions*	*Others*
160	24	16	5	3
Percentage	15	66.67	20.83	12.5

Source: Interview responses.

An attempt is also made in this study to present farm-size wise classification of sources of borrowers for repaying the loan. For this purpose it is important to know whether the borrowers under different farm-sizes are repaying the crop loan and business loan from the additional income obtained from the credit financed activity. The situation is presented in Table 5.21. Table 5.21 shows that 40.91 percent of the borrowers under small farmers category have refunded the loan from the additional income earned from the utilization of credit followed by marginal farmers (27.27 percent) medium farmers (22.73 percent) and agricultural labourer classes (9.09 percent)respectively whereas 62.50

percent of the borrowers under small farmers categories do not pay the debt from the additional income earned from the credit financed activity followed by agricultural labourer classes (29.17 percent) and marginal farmers (8.33 percent) respectively. The highest percentage of borrowers under marginal farmers (38.60 percent) are not hope-full of repaying the loan from the income likely to be earned from the credit financed activity followed by small farmers (35.09 percent), agricultural labourers (13.16 percent) and medium farmers (13.16 percent), respectively. It indicates that the large number of marginal farmers have probably misutilised the loan. It is also interesting to note that no borrower under medium farmers category have repaid the loan from the additional income obtained from the credit financed activity although 15 borrowers out of 20 respondents have obtained surplus income from the credit financed activity (Table 5.7)

Table 5.21 : Income Earned from Credit Financed Activity and Refund of Loan According to Farm Size

Farm Size	*No. of borrowers who repaid loan from the additional income earned from credit financed activity*	*No. of borrowers who paid the loan from other sources*	*No. of borrowers who do not expert to repay the loan from the income likely to be earned from credit financed activity*
SF	9(40.91)	15(62.50)	44(35.09)
MF	6(27.27)	2(8.33)	44(38.60)
MF*	5(22.73)	-	15(13.16)
AL	2(9.09)	7(29.17)	19(13.16)
Total	22(100)	24(100)	114(100)

Figures in the parentheses represent percentages.

Source: Interview Responses.

Table 5.22 shows the sources of refund other than income from the activity. Farm-size wise analysis (5.22) reveals that the highest percentage of borrowers under small farmers category have reported that raising loans from new types of gramine baniyas (mostly School teachers) are the main source used by them for repayment of loan. They represent 62.50 percent of the total number of borrowers. While the lowest percentage of borrowers (12.50 percent) under marginal farmers category have taken fresh loan from Jalpaiguri People's Co-operative bank for repayment whereas 100 percent of the borrowers under landless labourer classes have repaid the debt from other sources such as income from family members, borrowing from relatives etc.

Table 5.22 : Sources of Refund Other Than the Income From the Activity

Farm - size	*Other Sources*			
	Raising Loans from Baniyas	*Raising Loans from other institutions*	*Other*	*Total*
SF	10(62.50)	5(100)	-	15(62.5)
MF	2(12.50)	-	-	2(8.33)
MF*	-	-	-	-
AL	4(25)	-	3(100)	7(29.17)
Total	16(100)	5(100)	3(100)	24(100)

Source: Field Survey, 2006-07.

As regards the methods adopted by the farmers to repay their principal and interest, the item "other sources for repayment" plays significant role compared to income earned from credit financed activity. The field survey reveals that out of 160 respondents 22 borrowers (13.75 percent) depend on the additional income earned from the credit financed activity, on the other hand 24 borrowers (15 percent) make, a repayment out of the income earned from the loan based activity. Among other ways and means adopted for repayment, raising loans from new types of gramin baniyas plays a significant source to the borrowers under small farmers category (62.5 percent) followed by agricultural labourers (29.17 percent) and marginal farmers

(8.33 percent) respectively. The tendency of raising loans from other institutions is found to be high among the borrowers under small farmers category only and the study also reveals that the highest percentage of borrowers under landless labourer classes (cent percent) use income from other sources for repayment. The foregoing analysis of the sources for repayment reveals that out of 24 borrowers who have to depend on other sources for repayment 16 borrowers (66.67 percent) have managed to raise loans from informal sources of credit.

The study has found that the prompt and regular repayment of loan installments has largely occurred through cross financing and not through the returns from the investment under taken with the loan. This high levels of cross financing has depleted the capital of the loan and has reduced the value of the new loan that is used to repay the old. This process may lead to a "vicious cycle".

5.4.1 Extent of Overdues at Defaulter Level

The success or failure of any activity will be reflected to a considerable extent in the overdue loan installment position of the borrowers. In a sound functioning of any better recovery of loans and less amount of dues motivate the institution for more and more development financing in the area of operation of that institution. Repayment of loan in time is, therefore, considered as one of the prudent deployment of funds[7]. It is against this background that the present section is devoted to assessing an estimate of overdues at the farm level.

During field survey the data on principal and interest unpaid were collected by persuing the loan pass book and with the help of discussion with the borrowers. Based on the data so collected an effort has been made in this present section to get an estimate of overdues at the farm level. The distribution of defaulters on the basis of farm size is shown in Table 5.23. The average amount of over due per borrower is about Rs.8374.90 the range being Rs.4275.33 to Rs.16333.33.

The Table 5.23 also depicts the picture with regard to defaulters as proportion of borrowers. On an average the percentage of defaulters to borrowers is 71.25. Among the farm size groups, the percentage of defaulters to borrowers is the highest in the lowest category of farmers, followed by the highest category (Table 5.23).

Table 5.23: Overdues Position at Defaulter Level

	Defaulters			
Land Size Group	*No. of Respondents*	*Repaid in Part*	*Not Repaid at all*	*Average amount of overdue*
SF	64	42	2	7741.09
MF	52	32	8	7625.00
MF*	20	-	15	16333.33
AL	24	11	4	4275.33
All Groups	160	85	29	8374.90

Source : Field Survey, 2006-07.

It is the lowest for agricultural labourer classes (16.67 percent). A close look at Table 5.23 indicates that average amount of overdues per defaulter is the highest (Rs.16333.33) in the highest category of farm households, it is the lowest for the agricultural labourer classes (Rs.4275.33). From the Table 5.23 it is clear that per defaulter overdues have a tendency to increase with the increase in the size of holding.

The information about the percentage distribution of overdues among different category of farmers is presented in Table 5.24. Table 5.24 reveals that among the different category of farmers, the highest share in total overdues is reported by small farmers. They accounted for nearly 36 percent of the total overdues. The marginal farmers have the second highest share and it is about 32 percent. The share of overdues to total is the lowest for the agricultural labourer classes (6.72 percent). Among the different category of farmers, the highest share in total overdues is reported by small farmers. They accounted for nearly 36 percent of the total overdues. The marginal farmers have the second highest share and it is about 32 percent. The share of overdues to total is the lowest for the agricultural labourer classes (6.72 percent).

Table 5.24: Distribution of Overdues by Holding Size Categories

Farm Size	*Loan Overdues*
SF	35.68
MF	31.95
MF*	25.66
AL	6.72
All Group	100

Source: Field Survey, 2006-07.

A close look at Table 5.23 indicates that overdues form 63.37 percent of the outstanding debt. Amongst holding size groups, it is observed that the proportion of overdues to outstanding loans is the highest to the borrowers belonging to small farmers, followed by the agricultural labourers. The proportion is the lowest in the third holding size group of farmers. This clearly shows that the overdues problem is very serious in the case of marginal, small farmers and agricultural labourers. The diagrammatic presentation of overdues position of the borrowers in the district is given in Figure 5.4.

Figure 5.4
Overdues Position of Borrowers

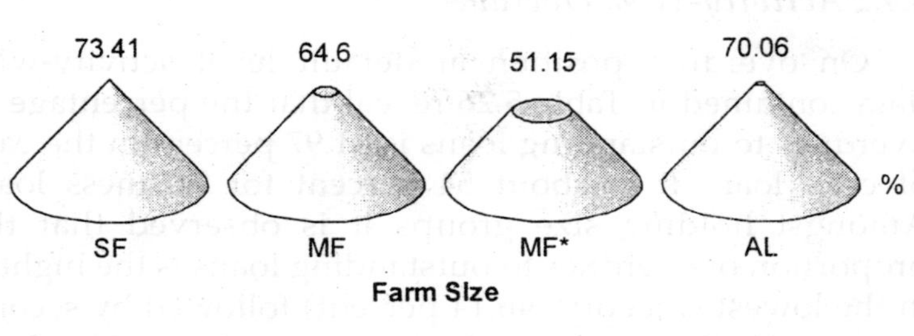

Table 5.25: Overdues as Percent of Outstanding Loans

Farm Size	At Defulter Level		
	Total outstanding Loan (Rs)	Total overdue	Overdues as % of loan outstanding
SF	463980	340608	73.41
MF	472120	305000	64.60
MF*	478950	245000	51.15
AL	91530	64130	70.06
Total	1506580	954738	63.37

Source: Field Survey, 2006-07.

Table 5.26: Activity-Wise Overdue Position of the Defaulters

Farm size	Crop Activity			Business Activity		
	Total outstanding loan	Total overdues	Overdues as % of loan outstanding	Total outstanding loan	Total overdues	Overdues as % of loan outstanding
SF	681155	305032	44.78	57725	35576	61.63
MF	495726	228750	46.14	118030	76250	64.60
MF*	678640	245000	36.10	-	-	-
AL	-	-	-	151248	64130	42.40
Total	1855521	778782	41.97	327003	175956	53.81

Source: Field Survey, 2006-07.

5.4.2 Activity-Wise Overdues

On overdues position at default level activity-wise data contained in Table 5.26 reveal that the percentage of overdues to outstanding loans is 41.97 percent in the case of crop loan. It is about 54 percent for business loan. Amongst holding size groups it is observed that the proportion of overdues to outstanding loans is the highest in the lowest category (46.14 percent) followed by second category (44.78 percent) in the case of crop loans. The share of overdues to outstanding loans is the highest in the lowest category (64.60 percent) followed by second category (61.63 percent) in the case of business loan also. For small and marginal farmer categories the share of overdues to outstanding loans in the case of business loan is more than that of crop loans. The diagrammatic presentation of overdues position at defaulter level (activity wise) is given in Figure 5.5.

Figure 5.5: Activity-Wise Overdues Position of Borrowers

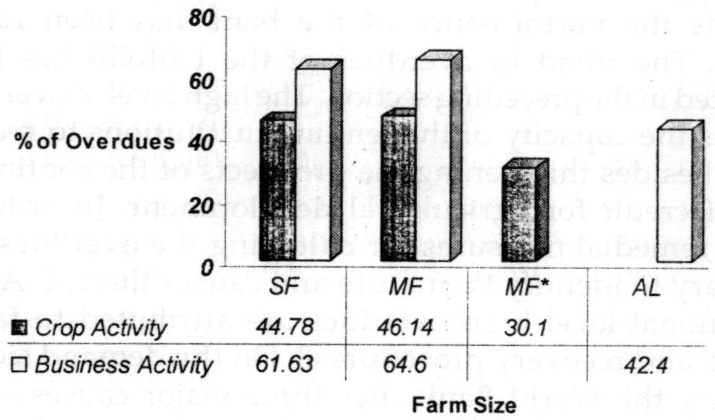

The foregoing description gives an account of the overdue position at defaulter level. The study shows that per defaulter the amount of overdues increases with the increase in holding size. It is the highest in the highest category of farmers and lowest for the agricultural labourer classes. The proportionate share of overdues is the highest for small farmers and lowest for agricultural labourer classes. The proportion of overdues to outstanding loan is considerably high in the case of marginal and small farmers respectively.

This may be due to low return from the activity on which the loan was disbursed by the UBKGB and also due to delay in granting credit.

In activity-wise analysis the percentage of overdues is high in the case of business loan compared to crop loan. It is observed form the study that though 114 respondents (71.25 percent) are defaulters, the principal and interest due that remains unpaid (63.37 percent) constitute a large amount. Hence the hypothesis that "there is high amount of overdues" is accepted.

5.4.3 Reasons for Default in Repayment of Loan

Credit disbursed by the UBKGB for the development of agriculture has made rapid strides over the last few years as noted in the chapter II. However, on the side of recovery of loans the performance of the bank has been rather dismal. The trend in overdues of the UBKGB has been presented in the preceding section. The high level of overdues restricts the capacity of the lending institutions to recycle funds, besides threatening the prospects of the continious flow of credit for agricultural development. In order to devise remedial measures for cultailing the overdues it is necessary to identify the nature and causes thereof. At the institutional level high overdues are attributed to faulty lending and recovery procedures8. On the demand side of overdues the World Bank cites three major causes – The failure of farmers to use borrowed funds for production, the failure of the investment and the refusal to repay9. This section is concerned with the analysis of the causes of overdues from the demand side only.

Iin order to ascertain the borrowers perceptions of the causality of defaults, interviewed 114 defaulters among three different blocks and the results are presented in the Table 5.27. The survey reveals that out of 160 respondents, 46 (28.75 percent) have repaid their principal and interest regularly and have no dues, while the remaining 114 (71.25 percent) are defaulters. The table shows that of the 114 defaulters 38.60 percent, 35.09 percent, 13.16 percent and 13.16 percent of the borrowers belong to small, marginal, medium farmers and agricultural labourers respectively. 45.46 percent, 40 percent and 33.33 percent of the borrowers are delinquent due to crop diseases.

Table 5.27: Borrowers' View of Causality of Default

Particulars	*SF*	*MF*	*MF**	*AL*	*No. of Borrowers*
1.Crop diseases	20(45.46)	16(40)	5(33.33)	-	41(35.96)
2.Inadequate income generation	5(11.36)	6(15)	-	7(46.67)	18(15.79)
3.Diversion of amount for other purposes	8(18.18)	4(10)	-	5(33.33)	17(14.91)
4. Poverty	4(9.09)	4(10)	-	3(20)	9(7.90)
5. Poor monitoring	2(4.54)	2(5)	-	-	6(5.26)
6. Do not know	5(11.36)	8(20)	10(66.67)	-	23(20.18)
Total	44(100)	40(100)	15(100)	15(100)	114(100)

Figure in the brackets represent percentages to total.

Source: Field Survey, 2006-07.

The table also shows that crop diseases and inadequate income generation from the activities for which loans are sanctioned are important reasons contributing to the problem of overdues. About 45.46 percent of borrowers under small farmers, 40 percent of borrowers under marginal farmers and 33.33 percent of borrowers under medium farmers fall under the first reason (crop diseases). Second reason for overdues viz inadequate returns from the activities, is the most prominent one in the case of agricultural labourers (46.67 percent), followed by marginal farmers (15 percent) and small farmers (10 percent) respectively. Diversion of credit for other puposes such health, education etc is reported as the third important reason for overdues by agricultural labourers (33.33 percent) followed by small farmers (18.18 percent) and marginal farmers (10 percent) respectively.

We also see from the table that the largest percentage of respondents i.e, 66.67 percent defaulters under medium farmers category, 20 percent under marginal farmers and 11.36 percent under small farmers category do not indicate any specific reason which has compelled them to default in repayment of dues to UBKGB. This is in fact a "Do not know" category. These types of defaulters are seemed to be wilful defaulters another 7.90 percent of borrowers have not refunded the loan due to poverty. Only a small proportion of borrowers have cited the poor monitoring as the cause of overdues. The proportion of borrowers stating this factor as reason for overdues are 4.54 percent and 5 percent under small and marginal farmer categories respectively.

The foregoing analysis of reasons for overdues reveals that the principal reason for overdues is the crop disease. Hence the hypothesis that "inadequate income from the loan based activity is the major reason for overdues" is rejected. In our study low return from the activities is the third important reason for overdues. Inadequate return from loan based activity is the next important reason for overdues as reported by the borrowers. Poor monitoring as a reason for overdues is reported only by a small proportion of borrowers (5.26 percent).

This chapter provides an account how 89.38 percent of the borrowers have utilised the agricultural loan for the required purposes and 10.62 percent do not utilise the loan for the scheduled productive purposes. The study reveals that 33.06 percent of the borrowers have misused the crop loan either partially or fully and 35.90 percent of the borrowers have misused the business loan. The percentage of improper utilisation of crop loan is high among the borrowers under medium farmers category (45 percent) whereas the percentage of improper utilization of business loan is high among the borrowers under marginal farmers category. Inadequacy of loan obtained is the major reason inducing the borrowers to misuse the loan obtained. Lack of proper supervision and untimely credit rank as the second and third reasons as stated by the borrowers for misuse of credit.

The repayment performance of the borrowers shows that only 28.75 percent have repaid the loan. The percentage of overdues is comparatively high among the borrowers under small farmers category (73.41 percent). From activity-wise overdue position we see that the percentage of overdues is comparatively higher in the case business activity (53.81 percent) than the crop activity (41.97 percent). From the sources of repayment of loan we have that 13.75 percent of borrowers have repaid their loans from income earned from credit financed activity and out of 86.25 percent 15 percent have reported that they do not pay the loans from the loan-based activity and remaining 71.75 percent do not expect to repay the loan from income likely to be earned from credit financed activity. Among other source adopted for repayment, raising loans from baniyas (mostly school teachers) play a significant role and this is followed by raising loans from other institutions. From the socio-economic study we have found that only sex of the beneficiaries is related to repayment performance. The study shows that the repayment performance is better in the case of female borrowers.

While analyzing the factors responsible for overdues we have found that the highest percentage ascribe their default due to the crop diseases. Inadequacy of loans is of immediate concern to the borrowers and constitute the next important factor for overdues followed by diversion of credit for other purpose. In the next chapter an attempt is made to study the impact of credit on the borrowers.

NOTES AND REFERENCES

1. S.K. Sinha (1992), *Recovery of Loans from Farmers*, Deep and Deep Publications, New Delhi
2. Bhupal Singh Negi (1990), *Co-operative Credit and Regional Development*, Deep and Deep Publications, New Delhi
3. During field survey we have found a new category creditors. They are mostly school teachers who give loans to the farmers and in return they get higher amount in cash or in kind just after harvest.
4. Dr. Benson Kunjukunju and Dr. S. Mohanan (2000), *Institutional Finance and Rural Development*, New Century Publications, New Delhi.

5. Maufred Zeller (1996), Determinants of Repayment Performance in Credit Groups: The Role of Program Design, Inter-Group Risk Pooling, and Social Cohesion in Madagascar. Research Report 13, Washington, D.C., International Food Policy Research Institute.
6. Balwinder Singh (2000), *Agricultural Credit, Sources, Problems and Emerging Issues*, Deep and Deep Publications, New Delhi.
7. Dr. Benson Kunjukunju and Dr. S. Mohanan, *op. cit*, p. 180.
8. A. Ranga Reddy (1990), *Agricultural Development Rural Credit and Problems of its Recovery*, Mittal Publications, New Delhi.
9. A. Ranga Reddy, *op. cit*, p. 105.

6

Impact of Agricultural Credit

6.1: Introduction

Economic development in real sense is possible only when development of the weaker sections takes place1. The weaker sections in India consist of small farmers, marginal farmers, agricultural labourers etc. With a view to achieving this economic development RRBs disburse credit to the rural people. It is natural that the banks expect the borrowers to make proper utilisation of credit. If the credit is utilised properly for the purposes for which it was sanctioned, its impact i.e, flow of benefit to the beneficiaries, will help in improving their economic status. Scientific use of credit creates additional employment opportunities, increases income of the borrowers and helps to increase their living standard.

The present study aims to find out the impact of the schemes financed by UBKGB on the economic conditions of the rural people. The aspects are detailed under three heads, viz., credit impact on employment, on income and on living standard of weaker sections taking credit from the UBKGB.

6.2 Impact of Credit on Self-Employment

The bank finance issued to the rural poor is aimed at the removal of unemployment through the generation of additional employment. In order to assess the benefits derived by the borrowers, required data have been collected from them on the number of months worked in a year at two points of time, viz. pre-loan and post loan periods. For analyzing the impact of credit on generation of employment, the average annual employment (in months) of the borrowers is worked out.

Table 6.1 shows a detailed picture relating to the employment position of borrowers alone at two points of time viz. pre-loan and post-loan periods. It can be seen from the table that before availing the credit the employment of the borrowers was for about 6 months in a year in the activity for which loan was taken. While in the post-loan period such employment is estimated as 7 months a year. The bank credit thus generates additional employment to the borrowers in the scheduled activity for months in a year representing a 21.75 percent increase over the period.

Table 6.1: Annual Employment Position of the Borrowers in the District(in month)

No of borrowers	*Average self employment pre-loan*	*Average self employment post-loan*	*Difference in employment*	*Percent change in employment*
160	6.078	7.4	1.322	21.75

Source: Sample Survey, 2006-2007

Now an appropriate significance test would allow us to know exactly whether the variation in the self- employment in the district from the loan based activity in the post loan period differs significantly over the pre loan period.

"t" test of significance has been selected for necessary appraisal. In order to apply the t-test the null hypothesis set up is H0 : There is no variation in self employment of the borrowers in the post loan period. From Table 6.2 it is clear that the calculated 't' value (4.156) is higher than the table value (1.96) at 5 percent level, which indicates that the variation in the self employment of borrowers is statistically highly significant.

Table 6.2 : Variation in the Self-employment of Borrowers

Statistics		*t-statistics for difference of mean*
Mean difference	1.322	4.156*
SD	4.0237	
Maximum	9.0	
Minimum	-10.0	
No of observations	160	

Note: *significant at 5 percent level.

Block-wise impact of credit on employment position of the sample respondents (table 6.3) shows that additional employment among the borrowers has invariably been generated in all selected villages under three blocks after availing the bank credit. The table shows that the rate of employment generation is the highest in two villages under Maynaguri block with 34.22 percent increase. The percentage in employment generation in the selected villages under Jalpaiguri sadar is 22.49 percent but the lowest increase is recorded in Rajganj block viz., 10.16 percent.

The table further shows that in the post loan period, on an average about 2 months of self employment has been generated additionally to the borrowers in two villages (combined) under Maynaguri block over the pre-loan period. While on an average about 1 month of self employment has been generated in the post loan period to the borrowers in combined two villages under Jalpaiguri sadar and it is about 0.67 months under Rajganj block.

The dispersions of the months of work among the selected villages under three blocks as measured by SD and CV are shown in the Table 6.4.

Table 6.3: Block-Wise Classification of Annual Employment Position of the Borrowers (in Months)

Block	*No of borrowers*	*Mean self employment per-loan*	*Mean self employment post-loan*	*Difference in employment*	*% change in employment*
Maynaguri	53	5.72	7.68	1.96	34.27
Jalpaiguri sadar	54	5.93	7.26	1.33	22.43
Rajganj	53	6.59	7.26	0.67	10.16

Source: Sample Survey, 2006-07

From the Table 6.4 we find that in Maynaguri block standard deviation(SD) has decreased from 3.152 to 2.914 and also in Jalpaiguri sadar and Rajganj block standard deviations (SD) have decreased from 3.213 and 3.393 to 3.211 and 3.001 respectively. The table further shows that there is large variation in self employment among the borrowers of Jalpaiguri sadar and little variation among the borrowers of Maynaguri block after availing the credit.

The diagrammatic presentation of impact of credit on self employment position of the sample borrowers among the selected villages is shown in Figure 6.1.

Figure 6.1: Impact of Credit on Self-Employment Position of Borrowers

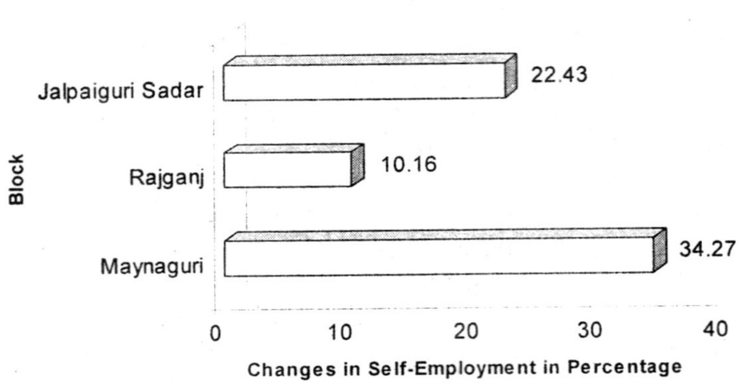

Table 6.4: Variation in Self employment Position of the Sample Borrowers

Blocks	*SD*		*CV*	
	Pre-loan period	*Post-loan period*	*Pre-loan period*	*Post period*
Maynaguri	3.152	2.914	55.105	37.943
Jalpaiguri sadar	3.213	3.211	54.182	44.229
Rajganj	3.393	3.001	51.487	41.336

Source: Sample Survey, 2006-07.

In order to test the variations in the self employment of the borrowers in the six selected villages, 't' test has been applied. The Table 6.54 show that the 't statistics' for difference of mean employment shows that there is a significant difference in self employment of the sample borrowers between pre-loan and post periods except in the selected villages under Rajganj block.

Table 6.5 : Annual Employment Position of the Borrowers in Six Selected Villages Under Different Blocks

Block	*Mean difference in employment*	*Standard deviation*	*'t' value*
Maynaguri			
Bhelbhela & Husludanga	1.962	0.5663	3.47*
Jalpaiguri sadar			
Choudhury Para & Danguajhar	1.333	0.5766	2.31*
Rajganj			
Kaluarbari & Mogha Para	0.670	0.5020	1.33**

*Significant at 5 percent level

**Not significant.

Source: Field Survey, 2006-07.

In order to test differences among more than two groups of data, where more than two means are involved in the analysis, the method of ANOVA has been selected for calculating variations. Now we have to test whether employment generation differs significantly among the villages under different blocks. For this purpose the null hypothesis of "no difference" in employment generation among the villages has been tested.

ANOVA results are presented in Table 6.6.

Table 6.6: F-Test

Sources of Variation	*df*	*MS*	*F*
Between the groups	2	22.139	1.374
Within the groups	157	16.114	

Since the observed value of F (viz.1.374) is less than table value at 0.05 level indicating that employment generations among the blocks are equal. Thus we can say that employment of the borrowers has been generated at an uniform rate among the blocks.

6.2.1 Employment Generation by Different Categories of Borrowers

The mean self employment from the loan based activity, difference in employment and percentage change in employment of the borrowers belonging to different land size groups in the selected villages under Maynaguri block are presented in table 6.7. It can be seen from the table that the additional employment has been generated among all the categories of farm size though its magnitude varies from one category to another. In the post loan period the mean annual increase in self- employment per farm size works out to be the highest of the borrowers belonging to medium farmers (4.83 months), followed by marginal farmers (1.875 months), small farmers (1.772 months) and lowest for agricultural labourers (1.34 months). While the percentage of increase in employment generation is the highest for borrowers belonging to medium farmers (120.75 percent), followed by marginal farmers (34.09 percent), small farmers

(30.22 percent) respectively, it is only 21.54 percent in the case of borrowers belonging to agricultural labourers. Table 6.7 further shows that mean self employment position of the borrowers under marginal farmers and agricultural labourers are not statistically significant at 5 percent level.

Table 6.7: Farm-Size wise Classification of Self-Employment position in the Selected Villages under Maynaguri Block

Farm size	*No. of borrowers*	*Mean self employment pre-loan*	*Mean self employment post*	*Difference in employment*	*% change in employment*	*t value*
SF	22	5.864	7.636	1.772	30.22	2.231*
MF	16	5.5	7.375	1.875	34.09	1.661
MF*	6	4	8.83	4.83	120.75	3.642*
AL	9	6.22	7.56	1.34	21.54	0.877

*Significant at 5 percent level

Source: Sample Survey, 2006-07

In order to test the variation in self-employment position among the farm sizes one-way ANOVA has been applied. From the table it is clear that the calculated value (1.307) is smaller than the table value at 5 percent level. So we accept the null hypothesis. This implies that the employment opportunities has been generated at an uniform rate among the farm sizes in two villages under Maynaguri block.

Table 6.8: One-way ANOVA

Source	*MS*	*df*	*F*
Between group	21.83	3	1.307
Within group	16.70	49	

Source: Sample Data, 2006-07

Table 6.9 shows that the details of the generation of additional employment of different farm sizes in Jalpaiguri sadar. It may be observed that in Jalpaiguri sadar, among the four farm categories that have received bank loans, the borrowers under agricultural labourers ranks first in the matters of employment generation (64.54 percent) followed by medium farmers (21.95 percent) and marginal farmers (17.88 percent)respectively. But the borrowers under small farmers category have recorded only 11.87 percent of additional self employment. The variation in self employment generation of the borrowers under agricultural labourer category is only statistically significant at 5 percent level.

Table 6.9: Farm Size-wise Classification of Self Employment Position in Two Selected Villages under Jalpaiguri Sadar

Farm size	*No. of borrowers*	*Mean self employment pre-loan*	*Mean self employment post-loan*	*Difference in employment*	*% change in employment*	*'t' value*
SF	17	5.206	5.824	0.618	11.87	0.744
MF	23	6.565	7.739	1.174	17.88	1.107
MF	6	6.833	8.333	1.5	21.95	0.946
AL	8	4.938	8.125	3.187	64.54	2.64*

*Significant at 5 percent level

Source: Sample Survey,2006-07

Now to test the employment generation among the all land size groups in two selected villages under Jalpaiguri sadar, ANOVA has been applied. ANOVA results are shown is table 6.10.

Table 6.10: ANOVA Results

Sources of variation	*Df*	*MS*	*F*	*Significant*
Between groups	3	5342632.22		
Within groups	50	2374705.03	2.250	0.094

Here calculated value of F is significant at 10 percent level. Hence the employment generation among the farm sizes in two selected villages under Jalpaiguri sadar has been created after availing bank loan.

Since F-ratio in ANOVA of data is significant at the given level, post Hoe test is used to uncover the group (s) contributing to the significant result. For this purpose the method considers contrast pairs among means.

Table 6.11: Multiple Comparisons for Testing Significance Contributed by Land Holding Groups in Selected Villages under Jalpaiguri Sadar

Farm size number(i)	*Farm size number(j)*	*Mean Difference (i-j)*	*Significant*
1.	2	-172.06	1.000
	3	179.35	1.000
	4	-1641.67	0.325
2.	1	172.06	1.000
	3	351.41	1.000
	4	-1469.61	.300
3.	1	-179.35	1.000
	2	-351.41	1.000
	4	-1821.01*	0.078
4.	1	1641.67	0.325
	2	1469.61	.300
	3	1821.01*	0.078

The mean difference is significant at 0.1 level. 1=AL, 2=SF, 3=MF,4=MF*

The Table 6.11 shows that contrast pair (3-4) or (4-3) is significant by post Hoc Test with 0.1.level. Thus the contrast pair (3-4) or (4-3) is contributing significantly in F ratio test, while other contrast pairs are insignificant.

Analysis of the impact of credit on employment creation between pre-loan and post-loan periods in two selected villages under Rajganj block is presented in table 6.12. It is clear that the borrowers belonging to agricultural labourers rank first in the matter of employment generation. After receiving the loan, the borrowers under agricultural labourer category could get an additional employment of 2.28 months representing 41.99 percent increase over pre-loan period. While in the post loan period, on an average only 0.08 months of self employment has been generated additionally to the borrowers belonging to small farmers. The borrowers under small farmers category have reported 1.18 percent rise in employment generation, while the borrowers belonging to marginal farmers and medium farmers have recorded 11.23 and 13.79 percent rise respectively. The variation in self employment generation of the borrowers belonging to agricultural labourers is only statistically significant at 5 percent level.

Table 6.12: Farm-Size-Wise Classification of Self Employment Position in Two Selected Villages Under Rajganj Block

Farm size	*No. of borrowers*	*Mean self-employment pre-loan*	*Mean self-employment post-loan*	*Difference in employment*	*% change in employment*	*'t' value*
SF	25	6.76	6.84	0.08	1.18	0.092**
MF	13	6.50	7.23	0.73	11.23	0.822**
MF*	8	7.25	8.25	1.00	13.79	0.921**
AL	7	5.43	7.71	2.28	4.99	3.053*

* Significant at 0.05 level

** Not significant

Source: Sample Survey, 2006-07.

But from the ANOVA results we see that the variations in self employment generation in two selected villages are equal to all land size groups as the calculated value of F(viz. 2.401) is less than the table value (2.60) at 5 percent level of significance. Hence the employment generation has also been created at an uniform rate among all farm size groups after availing the credit in two selected village under Rajganj block.

Table 6.13: ANOVA Results

Sources of variation	*df*	*MS*	*F*
Between groups	3	387013.47	2.401
Within groups	49	1493686.89	

Source: Sample Data,2006-07.

6.2.3: A Detailed Statement of Additional Employment Generation of Different Farm sizes in the District

A detailed picture relating to the farm-size wise employment position of the borrowers is presented in table 6.14. It can be seen that additional employment has invariably been generated among all categories of borrowers. In the post loan period the average annual increase in self employment per borrower works out to be the highest for medium farmers (2.3 months) followed by agricultural labourers (1.979 months), marginal farmers (0.805 months)respectively. The table also shows that the percentage of increase in employment generation is the highest for medium farmers (37.40 percent). The percentages increase in employment generation for agricultural labourers and marginal farmers are 34.05 percent and 20.56 percent respectively, but the lowest increase is recorded for small farmers (13.33 percent).

Table 6.14: Farm Size-wise Classification of Annual Employment Position of Sample Borrowers

Farm size	*No. of borrowers*	*Mean self employment pre-loan*	*Mean self employment post-loan*	*Difference in employment*	*% change in employment*	*'t' value*
AL	24	5.8125	7.7917	1.979	34.05	
SF	64	6.0391	6.8437	0.805	13.33	
MF	52	6.22115	7.50	1.279	20.56	
MF*	20	6.15	8.45	2.3	37.40	

Source: Sample Survey,2006-07

The dispersion of employment (in months) among the size groups of borrowers as measured by SD and CV is shown in Table 6.15.

The table shows that both SD and CV have decreased from the pre-loan period to post-loan period for all size groups of farmers. The table further shows that variability in months of work is the least among the borrowers belonging to medium farmers and the variability is large among the sample borrowers belonging to small farmers in the post-loan period.

Table 6.15: Co-efficient of Variations (CV) and Standard Deviations(SD) Among the Size Groups

Farm size	*SD*		*CV*	
	Pre-loan period	*Post- loan period*	*Pre-loan period*	*Post-loan Period*
SF	3.132	2.929	51.86	42.80
MF	3.380	3.196	54.33	42.61
MF*	3.100	2.781	50.40	32.91
AL	3.602	3.007	61.97	38.59

Source: Sample Data, 2006-07.

To test the variations in the self employment of the borrowers of different land holding groups, t test has been applied. The data on this aspect have presented in Table 6.16.

Table 6.16: Variation in Self-employment Position of Farm Size Groups

Farm size AL	*SF*	*MF*	*MF**	
Mean difference	1.979	0.805	1.279	2.3
Standard deviation(SD)	3.62	3.92	4.45	3.63
t statistics	2.679*	1.643**	2.074*	2.835*

*Significant at 5 percent level

** Not significant

The above analysis indicates that the bank finance extended to the rural poor has a little favourable impact on the employment pattern of the borrowers. The supply of credit has enabled the borrowers to generate an additional employment marginally to the tune of 1.322 months a year indicating 21.75 percent increase over the pre loan period. In the matter of additional self employment generation during post loan period, the borrowers belonging to medium farmers in Maynaguri block have benefited significantly.

This may be the outcome of proper utilisation of credit. But the borrowers belonging to agricultural labourers both in Jalpaiguri sadar and in Rajganj block are better placed in the generation of self- employment. This may be due to the fact that majority of them are engaged in agricultural works throughout the year and also they concentrate more on loan- based activity. Among the different farm size groups we find that the borrowers belonging to medium farmers and agricultural labourers are better placed in the matter of self- employment generation in the district.

The Table 6.16 shows that there is significant difference in self employment of the sample borrowers between pre-loan and post-loan periods except the borrowers under small farmer category at 5 percent level. The diagrammatic presentation of the impact of credit on self employment position of the different farm sizes is given in Figure 6.2.

Figure 6.2: Impact of Credit on Self-Employment Position

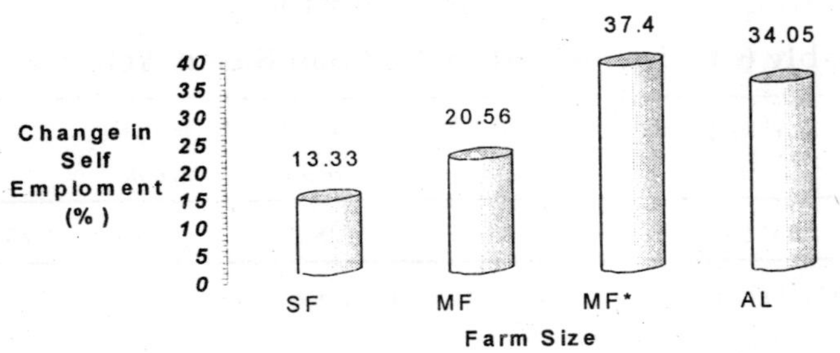

6.3 Impact of Credit on Income Generation

The aim of the bank finance issued to the rural poor is to remove poverty through generation of additional income opportunity and the resultant improvement in the standard of living. One of the main objectives of the present study is to find out the impact of loans on the income of the sample borrowers.

To assess the benefits derived by the borrowers, they were requested to supply informations relating to the net income obtained from the activity for which the loan was sanctioned at two points of time, viz., pre-loan and post-loan periods.

6.3.1 : Net Income from the Loan Based Activity

The mean income in the pre-loan and post-loan periods, difference in income and percentage change in income are presented in Table 6.17. It can be seen from the table that average annual income from the activity has increased from Rs.641.875 in the pre-loan period to Rs.770 in the post loan period resulting an increase in income of Rs.128.13 representing 19.96 percent increase over the pre-loan period. The overall increase of 19.96 percent in borrowers' net income appears to be insignificant. It is revealed from the table6.17 that the calculated value of 't' (1.237) is less than the table value(1.96) at 5 percent level of significance. It is thus inferred that the net income from the loan based activity of the borrowers in the pre-loan period does not differ from the net income in the post-loan period.

Table 6.17: Income from the Loan Based Activity

No. of Borrowers	*Mean pre-loan income*	*Mean Post-loan income*	*Difference in income*	*% change in income*	*'t' value*
160	641.875	770.00	128.13	19.96	1.237**

Note: ** Not significant at 5% level of significance.

Source: Sample Survey, 2006-07.

Block-wise classification of income from the loan based activity presented in table 6.18. reveals that the borrowers in all selected blocks have earned incremental incomes at the commencement of the post-loan period. Block-wise classification further shows that the highest mean incremental income from the loan-based activity is recorded in Maynaguri block (Rs. 218.87) and the lowest in Rajganj block (Rs.30.19). The percentage of increase in income over the pre-loan period also varies from a high of 29.87 percent in Maynaguri block to 24.01 percent in Jalpaiguri sadar and to a low of

4.78 percent in Rajganj block. The difference is not statistically significant in all the selected villages under three blocks. Now in order to compare the variability in annual income in selected villages after availing the credit co-efficient of variations are analysed. From the Table 6.19 it is clear that CV is high in Rajganj block followed by Jalpaiguri sadar and Maynaguri block respectively. Hence the disparity in annual net income in the post loan period is higher in Rajganj block than in Jalpaiguri sadar and Maynaguri block respectively.

Table 6.18: Classification of Income from the Loan Based Activity in the Selected Villages Under Different Blocks

(in Rs)

Block	*Mean pre-loan income*	*Mean Post-loan income*	*Difference in income*	*% change in income*	*'t' value*
Maynaguri					
Bhelbhela & Husludanga	732.68	950.94	218.87	29.87	1.576**
Jalpaiguri					
Choudhury Para & Danguajhar	562.96	698.15	135.19	24.01	0.623**
Rajganj					
Kaluarbari & Mogha Para	632.08	662.26	30.19	4.78	0.173**

** Not significant at 5% level of significance

Source: Sample Survey, 2006-07.

In order to test the variations of income among the villages under different blocks, one-way ANOVA has been used and the results are presented in table 6.20. As the calculated value is less than table value at 5 percent level of significance the null hypothesis namely that there is no significant difference in income among the selected villages is accepted. Thus it can be inferred from the table6.20 that the income in the post-loan period does not differ from the income in the pre-loan period. The block-wise impact of credit on income of borrowers is presented in Figure 6.3.

Figure 6.3: Impact of Credit on Income of Borrowers

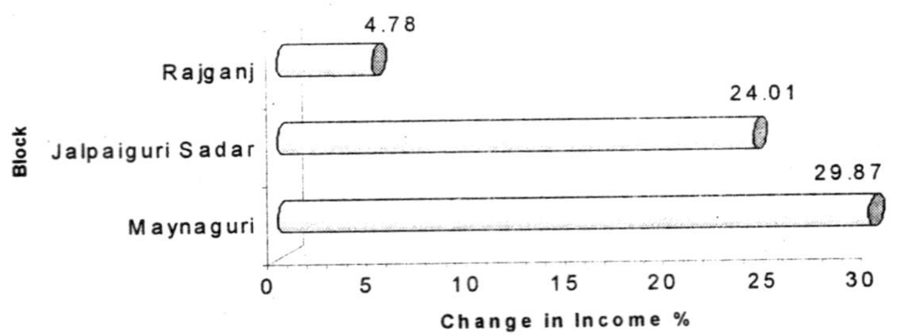

Table 6.19 : Co-efficient of Variations (CV) Among the Selected Villages under Different Blocks

Block	*CV before Scheme*	*CV after Scheme*
Maynaguri		
Bhelbhela & Husludanga	123.24	118.52
Jalpaiguri sadar		
Choudhuri Para& Danguajhar	175.62	158.27
Rajganj		
Kaluarbari & Mogha Para	145.23	158.98

Source: Sample Data, 2006-07.

Table 6.20 : ANOVA Results

Source of variation	*df*	*Sum of squares*	*Mean of squares*	*F value*
Between Group	2	947459.2	473729.58	0.274**
Within Group	157	2.72E+08	1731566.74	

** Not significant at 5% level of significance.

H0 : accepted.

6.3.2: Detailed Statement of Additional Income Generation by Different Categories of Borrowers

The farm size-wise classification of income of the borrowers in the pre-loan and post-loan periods is presented in table 6.21. It is apparent from the table that the highest incremental income (Rs.1100) as well as percentage increase in income (100.46) are recorded in the case of borrowers under medium farmer category. It is also clear that the impact of loan provided to the rural poor under agricultural labourer, small farmer and marginal farmer categories is not appreciable as the data indicate a negative growth rate of money income in the post loan period over the pre-loan period. As the calculated value of 't' (3.123) is greater than the table value (1.96) at 5 percent level, the difference is statistically significant only in the case of borrowers of medium farmers.

Table 6.21 : Farm-Size-Wise Classification of Income from the Loan Based Activity in Selected Blocks

(in Rs)

Farm size	*No. of Borrowers*	*Mean pre-loan income*	*Mean Post-loan income*	*Difference in income*	*% change in income*	*'t' value*
1.AL	24	429.17	416.67	-12.50	-2.91	-0.068
2.SF	64	515.38	511.54	-15.63	-3.03	-0.102
3.MF	52	682.81	667.19	-3.85	-0.56	-0.021
4.MF*	20	1095.00	2195.00	1100.00	100.46	3.123*

*Significant at 5 percent level

Source: Sample Survey, 2006-07

Table 6.22: Co-efficient of Variations Among Different Farm Sizes

Farm size	*CV in the pre-loan period*	*CV in the post loan period*
SF	182.17	182.86
MF	140.93	129.71
MF*	95.62	39.43
AL	146.32	181.77

Source: Sample Data,2006-07

The Table 6.22 reveals that variability in annual income is the least in the case of borrowers belonging to medium farmers category and the highest in the case of borrowers belonging to small farmers category in the post loan period. We can further observe from the table that CV has been decreased to 39.62 percent (after scheme) from 95.62 percent in the case of medium farmers and in the case of marginal farmers it has been also decreased to 129.71 percent (in the post loan period) from 140.93 percent. It means that variability has decreased after the scheme only in the case of marginal and medium farmers respectively.

Now to test the equality of mean incomes generation among farm sizes, one way ANOVA has been applied here. The results are presented in Table 6.23.

From the table it is clear that the calculated value of F is greater than the table value at 5 percent level of significance, the null hypothesis namely that there is no significant difference of mean incomes among the farm sizes is rejected and the alternative hypothesis is accepted. Thus the bank finance has altered the income of different farm groups.

Table 6.23: ANOVA Results

Sources of Variation	*Sum of squares*	*df*	*Mean Square*	*F*
Between Groups	21593581.73	3	7197860.58	4.470
Within Groups	251209855.77	156	1610319.59	

*Significant at 5 percent level.

Since F ratio in ANOVA of data is Significant at the given level, Post Hoc Test as described by Bonferroni has been used to identify the group(s) contributing to the significant result.

Table 6.24 : Comparison for Testing Significance Contributed by Land Holding Groups

Group	*Mean*	*N*
1.	-12.50	24
2.	-15.63	64
3.	-3.85	52
4.	1100	20

Contrast pair	*Mean Difference*	*SE*	*Significance*
A (1-2)	3.13	303.740	1.000
B (1-3)	-8.65	313.152	1.000
C (1-4)	-1112.50*	384.204	0.026
D (2-3)	-11.78	296.915	1.000
E (2-4)	-1115.63*	325.080	0.05
F (3-4)	-1683.46*	333.42	.000

* Significant at the 0.05 level.

Here the contrast pairs C, E and F are significant at 5 percent level indicating that group of medium farmers is different in the sample groups. The diagrammatic presentation of the impact of credit on income of farm sizes is given in Figure 6.4.

Figure 6.4: Impact of Credit on Income

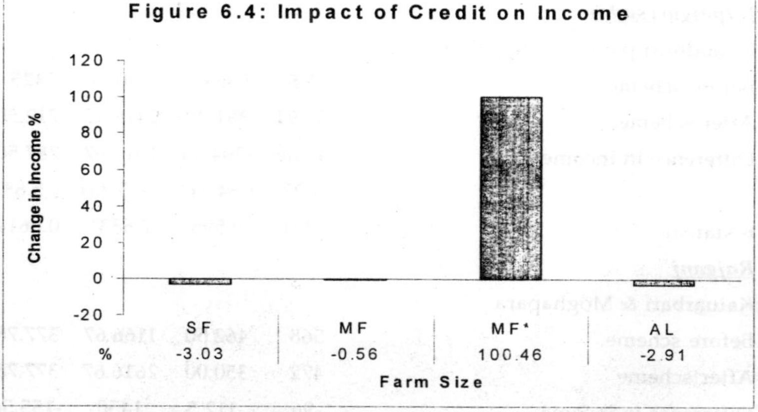

6.3.3 Block-wise Analysis of the Income Generation of Different Farm Sizes

Block-wise analysis of the income generation by different farm sizes is presented in table 6.25.

The table reveals that the income generation is negative for small farmer category in the selected villages under Maynaguri and Rajganj blocks but the income generation in the post-loan period is positive only in Jalpaiguri sadar. The mean incremental income of small farmers from the loan based activity in Jalpaiguri sadar is recorded at Rs.147.06 representing 24.27 percent increase over the pre-loan period.

Table 6.25: Classification of Mean incomes of Different Categories of Farm-size in Selected Blocks. (in Rs)

Block	*Farm size*			
	SF	*MF*	*MF**	*AL*
Maynaguri				
Bhelbhela & Husludanga				
Before scheme	872.73	262.50	1983.33	388.89
After scheme	822.73	750.00	2583.33	533.33
Difference in income	-50	487.50	600.00	144.44
	(-5.73)	(185.71)	(30.25)	(37.14)
t statistics	0.224	2.27*	1.024	0.543
Jalpaiguri sadar				
Choudhuri para& Denguajhar				
Before scheme	605.88	595.65	500	425
After scheme	752.94	391.30	2116.67	712.50
Difference in income	147.06	-204.35	1616.67	287.50
	(24.27)	(-34.31)	(323.33)	(-5.88)
t- statistic	0.391	0.595	2.633*	0.0614
Rajganj				
Kaluarbari & Moghapara				
Before scheme	568	462.50	1166.67	377.78
After scheme	472	350.00	2616.67	377.78
Difference in income	-96	-112.5	1450	-155.56
	(-16.90)	(24.32)	(124.28)	(-41.18)
t-statistic	0.412	0.828	1.718	0.685

Note: Figures in parentheses indicate percentage change

* Significant at 0.05 level

Source: Sample Survey,2006-07.

The income generation of marginal farmers is positive in the post-loan period only in Maynaguri block. The mean incremental income in this case is Rs.487.50 indicating a

185.71 percent rise over the average income in the pre-loan period. The income generation is positive only in the case of medium farmers in all selected villages under three blocks. The mean incremental income is the highest in respect of sample borrowers belonging to medium farmers in Jalpaiguri sadar (Rs. 1616.67) and it is the lowest in the case of medium farmers in Maynaguri block (Rs. 600). The mean incremental income of medium farmers in Rajganj block is Rs.1450. The percentage of increase in income over the pre-loan period also varies from a high of 323.33 percent in Jalpaiguri sadar block to 124.28 percent in Rajganj block and to a low of 30.25 percent in Maynaguri block. Similarly, the agricultural labourers are better placed in augmenting their income only in Maynaguri block. The borrowers under agricultural labourer category have received higher incremental income representing 37.14 percent rise over the pre-loan period.

In Maynaguri block, the rate of increase in income of the borrowers belonging to marginal farmers is as high as 185.71 percent and the calculated value of 't'(2.27) is higher than the table value at 5 percent level of significance, hence this difference in income is statistically significant. In Jalpaiguri sadar the mean incremental income of the borrowers belonging to medium farmers is the highest and the calculated value of t is greater than the table value hence this difference is also statistically significant and in Rajganj block differences in income of the borrowers under all categories of farm size groups are not statistically significant.

Thus it may be observed from the Table 6.25 that in Maynaguri block the marginal farmers have got the highest incremental income and in Jalpaiguri sadar, the medium farmers have received the highest incremental income. This may be due to credit discipline among the borrowers and also may be due to the much lower levels of income of these categories in the pre-loan period, which has resulted into a substantial increase in the post loan period. Thus the above situation has conclusively showed that the bank finance has a favorable impact only on the level of income of the beneficiaries belonging to marginal farmers and medium farmers in Jalpaiguri and Maynaguri blocks respectively. But in general the impact of credit on income does not present an encourasing result in the district. The survey reveals that borrowers have not augmented their mean incomes from the loan based activity by a reasonably good margin (19.96 percent) over the pre-loan period. The average income from the loan based activity has increased by Rs 128.13 over the pre-loan period. The borrowers in Maynaguri block have recorded the highest incremental income representing only 29.87 percent increase over the pre-loan period. The farm-size wise analysis shows that borrowers under medium farmers are better placed in augmenting their income levels, representing 100.46 percent rise over the pre-loan period. The high percentage of income accruing to the borrowers belonging to medium farmer category may be due to credit discipline among them and also the use of more inputs in production pattern which have increased the productivity. It may also be observed that in Jalpaiguri sadar small farmers have got the highest incremental income and they have got the lowest incremental income in Rajganj block. In Maynaguri block marginal farmers have got the highest incremental income and have received the lowest incremental income in Jalpaiguri sadar. While in Jalpaiguri sadar medium farmers have received the highest incremental income and they have got the lowest incremental income in Maynaguri block. Similarly the agricultural labourers have received the highest incremental income in Jalpaiguri sadar and have received the lowest in Rajganj block. Thus it is clear that there exists inter-block inequality in income even after the implementation of schemes.

6.4 Impact of Credit on Standard of Living

The main focus of economic planning is to raise the living standards of people who are living particularly below the poverty line[2]. The Regional Rural Banks (RRBs) were set up in 1975 with the objective of financing the credit requirements exclusively to the poorer sections. These RRBs can form the ideal institutional pattern to act as the agents of economic and social changes because they can bring these poorer sections within a common fold. The RRBs by providing adequate credit facilities to small and marginal farmers on liberal terms are playing a significant role in removing poverty and in raising living standard of the people[3].

This present section aims to find out the impact of credit on the living standard of the borrowers after availing the credit. The variables considered for analysis here are clothing, education to children, development of houses and recreational facilities such as use of T.V. In this context three terms have been used in this analysis. These are not improved, slightly improved and improved

In order to measure the improvement in the living standard the sample borrowers were asked to supply informations regarding above four variables and three code numbers are assigned to the three terms. A weight of 1 is given for not improved while a weight of 2 is given for slightly improved and a weight of 3 is given for improved. All these code numbers are added and the scores upto and inclusive of four are considered as indicative of not improved in standard of living. If the scores are between 5 to 11, it is assumed that living standard has slightly improved and if the score is 12 it is assumed that the standard of living of the borrowers has improved. Here "chi-square" test has been used to test the significance of variations between the selected villages and farm-sizes under different blocks.

It is clear from table 6.26 that there is no a significant change in the living standard of the borrowers in the study area. Only 9.38 percent of the borrowers have stated that their living standards have improved after availing credit. About 20.62 percent of the borrowers have reported that their standard of living have changed slightly while majority of the borrowers i.e, 70 percent of them have stated that they experience no increase in their living standard in the post-loan period.

Table 6.26: Impact of Loans on Standard of Living of Sample Borrowers

Standard of Living	*No of Borrowers*	*Percent to total*
1. No improvement	112	70.00
2.Slightly improved	33	20.62
3.Improved	15	9.38
Total	160	100

Source: Interview Responses

A close look at table 6.27 (village-wise classification) indicates that the analysis does not present encouraging results as only about 28.30 percent of the borrowers in the selected villages under Maynaguri block have experienced enhancement in their living standard, the corresponding percentages in Jalpaiguri sadar and Rajganj block are 18.52 percent and 15.09 percent respectively.

Table 6.27 : Classification of Impact of Loan on the Standard of Living in the Selected Villages under Different Blocks

Standard of Living	*Maynaguri Block Churabhander and Husludanga (Combined)*	*Jalpaiguri sadar Choudhuri Para and Denguajhar (Combined)*	*Rajganj Block Kaluarbari and Mogha Para (Combined)*	*Total*
No improvement	30(56.61)	40(74.07)	42(79.24)	112(70)
Slightly improved	15(28.30)	10(18.52)	8(15.09)	33(20.62)
Improved	8(15.09)	4(7.41)	3(5.67)	15(9.38)
Total	53(100)	54(100)	53(100)	160(100)

χ^2 =7.402, df=4

Figures in brackets represent the percentage of each item to row total.

Source: Interview Responses

From the table it is clear that 15.09 percent of the borrowers in Maynaguri block, 7.41 Percent borrowers in Jalpaiguri sadar and about 5.67 Percent borrowers under

Rajganj block have a clear increase in their living standards as compared to pre-loan period. As the calculated value of Chi-square (7.402) is less than the critical value (9.48), the village wise variations do not seem to exist any real difference in standard of living. The village-wise analysis reveals that the borrowers in the selected villages under Maynaguri block are better placed in improving the standard of living.

Farm size wise impact of credit on the living standard is presented in table 6.28.The table shows that significant difference only exists in the increase in living standard of the borrowers under medium farmers. In the case of medium farmers only 40 percent of the sample respondents have reported an increase in their living standard after availing credit.

Table 6.28 : Category-wise Classification of Impact of Loans on the Standard of Living

Standard of Living	*Farm size*				*Total*
	SF	*MF*	*MF**	*AL*	
Not Improved	48(75)	39(75)	9(45)	16(66.67)	112(70)
Slightly Improved	10(15.62)	9(17.31)	8(40)	6(25)	33(20.62)
Improved	6(9.38)	4(7.69)	3(15)	2(8.33)	15(9.38)
Total	64(100)	52(100)	20(100)	24(100)	160(100)

?2=14.94; df=9, Critical value at 5% level =16.919

Figures in the brackets indicate the percentage of each item to row total.

Source: Interview Responses.

But those borrowers whose standard of living have improved significantly constitute only 15 percent of the borrowers belonging to medium farmers followed by small farmers (9.38 percent), agricultural labourers (8.33 percent) and marginal farmers (7.69 percent) respectively.

The Chi-square (χ^2) test shows that χ^2 (observed) < ?20.05, 9 and hence at 5% level of significance H0(null hypothesis) is accepted. Hence there does not seem to exist any difference in standard of living of different farm groups after availing the credit.

From the foregoing analysis on the impact of credit on standard of living it can be concluded that the credit disbursed by the UBKGB has not a positive impact on the living standard of the sample borrowers.

On the standard of living of the sample respondents it is observed that about 70 percent borrowers do not observe any increase in their living standard after availing loans. From village-wise analysis we see that more than 50 percent borrowers in two villages under Maynaguri block and more than 70 percent of borrowers in other four villages under two blocks have reported that they experience no increase at all in their standard of living since availing themselves of credit facilities. Similarly the category-wise classification reveals that majority of the borrowers belonging to small farmers, marginal farmers and agricultural labourers do not observe a definite improvement in their living standard in the selected villages. The study reveals that the provision of bank finance help generate additional employment marginally in the district. The present study reveals that there is a 21.75 percent increase in self-employment on an average during the period subjected to study. As regard self- employment generation in the six selected villages, the borrowers of two villages (combined) under Maynaguri block (34.27 percent) have recorded benefit compared to other four villages under Jalpaiguri sadar and Rajganj block respectively. We also see that the borrowers belonging to medium farmers (37.40 percent) are better placed in regard to employment generation.

The impact of credit on net income of the borrowers indicates that on an average the borrowers have augmented his net annual income from the loan-based activity by a small margin of 19.96 percent compared to pre-loan period. Among the six selected villages, the borrowers of two selected villages namely Bhalbhala and Husludanga under Maynaguri block have the highest increase in net income (29.87 percent) in the post-loan period. Among the farm-sizes the borrowers belonging to medium farmers only have the highest net income (100.46 percent) in the post loan period.

Thus the impact of credit on the standard of living does not present encouring results. 70 percent of borrowers have experienced no improvement in their standard of living after utilisation of credit. In this regard only 9.38 percent of borrowers in six selected villages have a clear increase in their standard of living as compared to pre-assistance period. From category-wise classification we see that only the borrowers under medium farmers have shown somewhat improvement (55 percent) in their standard of living after availing credit. Hence the hypothesis that "there is no significant improvement in self-employment, income and standard of living of the borrowers" is accepted.

NOTES AND REFERENCES

1. A. Raja Rao, "Impact of the RRBs on Income and Employment of Weaker Sections", *Kurukshetra*, July 1996.
2. Dr. Benson Kunjukunju and Dr. S. Mohanan, *Institutional Finance and Rural Development*, New Century Publications, New Delhi, 2002.
3. Bhupal Singh Negi, *Co-operative Credit and Regional Development*, Deep and Deep Publications, New Delhi, 1990.

7

Conclusions

After going through the last six chapters of this study, we get a fairly detailed outlook of the manner in which UBKGB has emerged as a pioneering institution to provide credit to the weaker sections of the society in Jalpaiguri district of West Bengal. The study has tried to analyse the position of UBKGB in developing the rural areas of the district of Jalpaiguri because the bank was established with a specific objective to provide credit facilities to a particular section of the society.

The availability of banking and credit facilities is an essential input for the development of the rural masses and the subsequent elimination of money lenders. Since independence a number of institutions have been set up to provide credit to the rural poor to achieve the main objective of our national policy, viz., "development through credit". The Regional Rural Banks have now become a powerful instrument for economic development and they undertake the commendable task of providing credit to the rural people for agriculture and allied activities.

The present study is an attempt to evaluate the role of UBKGB, a Regional Rural Bank, in the development of the weaker sections in the district of Jalpaiguri, West Bengal.

The focus of the study is on a review of the progress of UBKGB in agricultural lending. It also makes an assessment of the credit deficiency, cost of borrowing credit, repayment performance, overdue position and impact of credit. The major findings of this study may be summarized in the following manner.

7.2 Agricultural Credit and UBKGB

By and large UBKGB has made considerable progress in lending to the agricultural sector. The agricultural credit in Jalpaiguri district has increased from the level of Rs. 60.96 lakhs in 1998-99 to Rs. 805.57 lakhs in 2006. It has increased by 13.2 times between 1998-99 and 2005-06 registering a compound growth rate of about 24.11 percent. The target share of credit of the bank under direct finance is 80.48 percent and achievement is 83.62 percent over the period 2002-06 while the credit share under allied activities has rapidly decreased both in terms of target (19.52 percent) as well as achievement (16.38 percent) over the same period. We also see that the overall achievement (68.45 percent) under direct finance is better than that of allied activities (55.29 percent) over the period 2002-06. This indicates the success of the bank's policy of extending direct assistance to agriculture.

The UBKGB has not only been engaged in development agriculture but it is playing a significant role in extending finance to the weaker section namely SC, ST and OBC population. UBKGB has sanctioned agricultural loans to SC population from Rs. 219.86 lakhs in 2004 to Rs. 477.51 lakhs in 2006 representing an increase of 61.40 percent whereas the advance sanctioned by the UBKGB to ST population has increased from Rs. 30.05 lakhs to Rs. 61.55 lakhs over the same period registering an increase of 61.76 percent. Further it has been observed that the loan sanctioned by the UBKGB to the SC, ST and OBC population has increases from 80.55 percent in 2004 to 93.96 percent in 2006 whereas the loan sanctioned to higher caste has decreased from 19.44 percent in 2004 to 12.74 percent in

2006. Thus the UBKGB is playing a significant role in extending credit to the weaker sections of the rural villages.

7.3 Sample Profile

The examination of the data obtained from the survey reveals that more than three-fourths of the sample borrowers are males and 42.62 percent of them are in the age group of 15-40 years. The caste wise classification shows that 53.75 percent of the sample borrowers is from SC/ST categories and 46.25 percent of the respondents is from forward castes. Family size is considered as one of the detriments for socio-economic development. Nearly 68.12 percent of the borrowers have three to five members in their family and the percentage of really large family sizes is quite low.

The level of education of the sample borrowers shows that 41.87 percent of the borrowers have no formal education and 39.38 percent of the sample borrowers have education level upto primary. An analysis made in relation to size of land holdings of sample borrowers indicates that 32.5 percent of loanees are having less than 2.5 acres of land and 40 percent of the borrowers are having 2.5-5 acres of land. The main occupational status of the borrowers shows that 75.62 percent of the borrowers are engaged in agricultural activities and 24.38 percent of borrowers depends other than cultivation.

7.4 Credit Needs of the Borrowers and Their Fulfillment

An estimation of the mean credit gap of the sample borrowers reveals that the UBKGB has failed to meet the credit needs of the rural poor to the extent of Rs. 8283.06 per borrower. It represents that more than one third (33.55 percent) of the credit requirements of the borrowers are not met by the UBKGB.

Village-wise analysis shows that the credit gap ranges from 39.83 percent in Jalpaiguri sadar to 22.53 percent in Rajganj block. The percentage of credit requirements remaining unfulfilled is high in the case of the borrowers under small farmers (79.91 percent) followed by medium farmers (50.84 percent), marginal farmers (26.54 percent) and agricultural labourers (23.32 percent). The credit requirements remaining unfulfilled is high in the case of borrowers under small farmers (47.68 percent) in Maynaguri block, it is high in the case of borrowers under medium farmers (66.56 percent) in Jalpaiguri sadar and the percentage of inadequacy of credit is also high in the case of agricultural labourers (38.02 percent).

7.5 Time Taken by UBKGB in Disbursing Loans

An analysis of the total amount of time spent by the borrowers in getting credit represents that majority of the borrowers (67.50 percent) get the loan sanctioned and disbursed within a period of 7 days from the date of application. As against this 28.75 percent of the borrowers have to wait for a period of 8 to 14 days and about 3.75 percent of the borrowers have to wait for a period of 15 to 30 days. The average time taken by the bank to disburse loans to the borrowers works out to 9 days. Block wise analysis on this aspect shows that the average time lag in getting credit is the highest in Maynaguri block (7.60 days) and the lowest in Jalpaiguri sadar (5.42 days). The average time lag in getting credit is the lowest in the case of medium farmers (5.17 days) in Maynaguri block and it is the lowest in the case of marginal farmers in Rajganj block and the average time taken in getting credit is the lowest in the case of small farmers in Jalpaiguri sadar.

7.6 Cost of Borrowing Credit by the Sample Borrowers.

An examination of the cost of borrowing credit shows that on an average a borrower has to spend Rs. 426 for obtaining the loan. This amount is equivalent to 2.6 percent of the loan amount. The borrowers in the selected villages under Maynaguri block have to incur 2.76 percent of the loan amount as borrowing cost. The percentage is as low as 2.29 percent under Jalpaiguri sadar. The borrowers belonging to marginal farmers incur a lower borrowing cost (2.36

percent) of the loan amount under Rajganj block and the borrowers belonging to medium farmers incur lower borrowing cost under Maynaguri block(1.39 percent) and Jalpaiguri sadar (1.6 percent). Overall the borrowers belonging to agricultural labourers incur a higher borrowing cost (3.85 percent) while the borrowers belonging to medium farmers incur the lowest borrowing cost (1.51 percent) in the district

7.7 Farmers' Experience with Bank Loans.

The borrower in getting loans from the banks faces many problems like attitudes and behaviour of the bank staff. UBKGB is not exception to this. A borrower who faces a large number of problems in getting credit may develop a retaliatory attitude towards the repayment of loan. This may cause overdues with the bank. This results in curbing a smooth flow of credit to the weaker sections of the villages.

While analyzing the problems connected with the bank it becomes evident that recommendation of panchayat pradhan for sanction of loan is the foremost problem faced by the borrowers. Delay in sanctioning loan and complicated loan procedure are ranked as the second and third major problems faced by them.

It is found that delay in sancting loan and recommendation of panchayat pradhan are the major problems faced by the borrowers in Maynaguri, Jalpaiguri sadar and Rajganj blocks respectively. Delay in sanctioning credit ranks the first among the problems faced by the borrowers under small farmers and agricultural labourers, recommendation of panchayat pradhan is the main problem for the borrowers under marginal and medium farmers.

Analysing the financial problems faced by the borrowers high borrowing cost of credit ranks as the first problem followed by loss of wages which is ranked as problem number two. High borrowing cost incurred is the major problem for the borrowers in Maynaguri block. But in Jalpaiguri sadar and Rajganj block loss of wages is the major problem. From farm size- wise we see that high borrowing cost incurred is the major problem for the borrowers under small, marginal farmers and agricultural labourers respectively. But loss of wages is ranked as the first problem of the borrowers under medium farmers.

7.8 Utilisation of Loan, Repaying Capacity and Repayment Performance of Borrowers

Banking services are of crucial importance in the transfer of capital to the weaker sections of the society. Care must be taken to ensure that credit is used effectively to create wealth and prosperity. The economic development in real sense can take place if credit is actually used for the purposes for which it is meant. Such credit, if used for a productive purpose will generate sufficient incomes not only support livelihood of the rural families obtaining credit but also yield surpluses which will help the borrowers to repay the loans promptly.As per the findings based on survey, 106 borrowers out of 143 have fully utilised the loan for the required purpose and the remaining 37 borrowers out of 143 have partially spent the loan on consumption items. It can be simply deducted thlat 17 borrowers (10.62 percent) do not fully utilise the loan for intended purposes and 37 borrowers have partially utilised the loan for the required purposes. Deducting the addition of the number of the users among the borrowers, it can be concluded that 54 borrowers out of 160 (33.75 per cent) do not utilise the loan for the required purposes. The percentage of borrowers who misused the loans obtained is the highest is the case of business loans (36 percent) and the lowest in the case of crop loans (33 percent). The percentage of borrowers who have misused the loans obtained is the highest in the case of business loans (36 percent) and the lowest in the case of crop loans (33 percent). The percentage of the borrowers who have misused the crop loans varies from a high of 45 percent is the case of borrowers under medium farmers to a low of 25.42 percent in the case of borrowers belong to small farmers. Whereas the borrowers who haved misused the business loans obtained varies from a high of 50 percent in the case of borrowers belonging to marginal farmers to a low of 29 percent in the case of borrowers under agricultural labourers.

7.8.1 Reasons for Misutilisation of Loans

The study reveals that out of 160 sample borrowers 54 respondents (33.75 percent) have misused the loans availed by them. Nearly 26 percent of the borrowers out of those misusing the credit state that inadequacy of credit is the reason compelling them to divert the loan amounts. About 19 percent have diverted the loan amounts due to lack of proper supervision and 17 percent have diverted the loan for untimely credit.15 percent of the borrowers misusing the credit report that poverty is the reason compelling them to divert the loan amounts.

7.8.2 Repaying Capacity and Repayment Performance of the Sample Borrowers

It is generally believed that repayment performance will be good if the activities undertaken happen to generate sufficient income. The repayment capacity depends upon the returns from the activity or business in which the debtor is engaged. A close analysis of primary data indicates that 36 percent, 40 percent and 75 percent of the borrowers belonging to small, marginal and medium farmers have achieved surplus income from the crop loans. Whereas from business loan 80 percent, 30 percent and 38 percent of the borrowers belonging to small farmers, marginal farmers and agricultural labourers have achieved surplus income. Thus we see from our study that the small farmers have been benefited most from business loans and the borrowers belonging to medium farmers have been benefited significantly from the crop loans.

7.8.3 Repayments of Loans and Overdue Position

The success of financing different activities depends on the borrowers' capacity to repay their loans regularly so as to enable the banks to further recycle of funds. This recycling of funds is seriously threatened by the tendency of the borrowers not to repay the loans. Hence the loan repayment with interest by borrowers is necessary for the smooth functioning of institutional credit system. A close analysis of the primary data indicates that of the total size of 160 sample borrowers, 29 percent of the borrowers have repaid in full while 53 percent of the borrowers have repaid part of the loan and remaining 18 percent of the borrowers have not repaid the loan at all. Further we find from our study that improvement in percentages of full repayment of loan is noticed in the case of the borrowers belonging to agricultural laborers (37.5 percent)

From repayment performance of loan amount by the borrowers we also find that about 37 percent of the principal and interest demanded by the UBKGB is paid by the borrowers and the balance 63 percent demanded is due from them. The average amount of overdues of the sample borrowers works out to Rs. 5967.

The percentage of principal and interest demanded but remains unpaid is the highest to the borrowers belonging to small farmers (73.41 percent) and the lowest to the borrowers belonging to medium farmers (51 percent). It can also be seen from the activity wise analysis that the percentage of overdues is high is the case of business loan (54 percent) compared to crop loan (42 percent).

The percentage of overdues in the case of business loan is more among the borrowers belonging to marginal farmers (65 percent) whereas the same is more among the borrowers belonging to marginal farmers in the case of crop loan (46 percent).

7.8.4 Source of Repayment

As regards the sources utilised for the repayment of loans, the survey reveals that about 14 percent of the borrowers have repaid their loans by utilizing the income from the loan based activity itself. 15 percent of the borrowers have reported that their income form the credit based activity is not sufficient for repayment and hence the income they could generate from other sources and their family members are used for repayment of principal and interest. Out of 24 borrowers 66.67 percent of them have taken loans from grameen baniyas,20.83 percent have managed to raise loans from other banks for the repayment of loan instalments and another 12.5 percent have repaid the loan from son's money order income from secondary occupation. 71 percent of the borrowers are not hopeful of repaying the loan from the income likely to be earned from the credit financed activity. It indicates that they either misuse the loan or circumstances force them to do so. nearly 41 percent of the borrowers belonging to small farmers, 27 percent of them under marginal farmers, 23 percent of medium farmers and 9 percent of agricultural laborers have repaid their loans by generating income from loan based activity.

7.8.5 Reasons for Overdues

About 16 percent of the defaulting borrowers find that income from the loan based activity is not sufficient for repayment of dues in time. Nearly 36 percent of them inform that crop disease is the main reason for their overdues. Nearly 15 percent of borrowers report that diversion of amount for other purpose is the major reason for overdues also. About 8 percent of the borrowers say that due to poverty they do not repay the loans and about 20 percent do not indicate any specific reason for doing so.

From farm size-wise analysis we find that about 45 percent of borrowers under small farmers state that crap disease is the main reason for overdues and 40 percent of them belonging to marginal farmers state the same reason. Whereas 67 percent of the borrowers under medium farmers do not indicate any specific reason for not repaying the loan. Thus while analysing the factors responsible for overdues we find that the highest percentage of borrowers ascribe their default due to crop diseases and 'do not know' is of immediate concern to the borrowers and constitute the next important factor for overdues followed by inadequacy of income from loan-based activity.

7.9 Impact of Credit on Employment

One of the main objectives of the bank finance is the generation of employment from the credit based activities. As per the findings based on survey the present analysis indicates that bank credit has no favourable impact on the self employment position of the borrowers. The average number of months of employment of borrowers has increased from about 6 months in the pre-loan period to about 7 months in the post-loan period. This represent a 21.75 percent increase over the period. Among the blocks the highest rate of self employment generation is recorded in Maynaguri block (34.27 percent) and the lowest in Rajganj block (10.16 percent). The average annual self-employment generation during the post-loan period is recorded to be the highest among the borrowers under medium farmers (37.40 percent) and the lowest to the small farmers (13.33 percent). Further from our study we find that the average annual self employment generation during the post-loan period is the highest among the borrowers under medium farmers (120.75 percent) in Maynaguri block and in Jalpaiguri sadar it is the highest among the borrowers belonging to the agricultural labourers (64.54 percent) and in Rajganj block the average annual self employment generation during the post loan period is recorded to be the highest among the borrowers belonging to agricultural labourers (42 percent) also.

7.10 Impact of Credit on Income

The primary objective of bank finance to the rural borrowers is the generation of additional income from credit based activities. The present study reveals that income generation during the post-loan period does not show any encouraging picture. The average net income from the loan based activity of the borrowers rises from Rs. 642 to Rs. 770, resulting in a net increase of Rs. 128.13 (19.96 percent) in the post-loan period compared to the pre-loan period.

Block wise classification shows that the highest mean incremental income from the loan-based activity is recorded in Maynaguri block (Rs. 219) and the lowest in Rajganj block (Rs. 30.19). From the percentage of increase in income we find that it also varies from a high of 30 percent in Maynaguri block to 24 percent in Jalpaiguri sadar and to a low of 5 percent in Rajganj block.

The farm size-wise analysis shows that borrowers under medium farmers are in a better place in augmenting their income levels because100.46 percent increase over the pre-loan period has been recorded of such borrowers. It is also observed from the study that in Jalpaiguri sadar the borrowers under medium farmers have got the highest incremental income (323.33 percent) and in Rajganj block medium farmers also have got the highest incremental income (124.28 percent). In Maynaguri block it is found that the marginal farmers usinging credit from UBKGB have the got the highest rate of growth of net income (186 percent).

7.11 Impact on Standard of Living

The survey reveals that there is no general improvement in the living standard of the borrowers. It is observed from the study that 70 percent of borrowers do not experience any improvement in their standard of living. Only 9 percent of the borrowers inform that there is significant improvement in their living standard. The rest 21 percent of the sample borrowers report that their living standard has slightly improved. The percentage of borrowers having no change in standard of living is the highest in Rajganj block (79 percent) and the lowest in Maynaguri block (57 percent) The category wise classification reveals that 75 percent of small farmers, 75 percent of marginal farmers and 67 percent of agricultural labourers are found to have no improvement in their living standard.

7.12 Suggestions

Keeping in views the foregoing findings of the study certain suggestions may be offered which would be useful for policy makers. The following suggestions are made on the basis of findings of the survey at the time of interview and opinions expressed by the sample borrowers:

1. The present method of provision of credit needs to be streamlined. The prompt decision in sanctioning the loans to the farmers should be conveyed to them by the bank so as to avoid unnecessary harassment, frequent visits to the bank and loss of time resulting in loss of wages.
2. It has been observed that the loan sanctioned is often inadequate to fulfil the purpose for which loan is applied and the borrowers, therefore, misutilise the borrowed amount for some other purposes. This fact has been disclosed by some borrowers during interview with them. Therefore, it may be suggested that the bank should provide adequate amount of loans to the borrowers to meet the purposes for which the loan is applied to prevent misutilisation of the amount.
3. It has also been found that there is a wide gap between the date of application for loan and date of granting it. Meanwhile the borrowers are compelled to borrow loan with higher rate of interest from the gramin baniyas to meet their immediate requirements. As a consequence, on receipt of the loan from the bank after a long period the borrowers repay the loan in the forms of principal amount with interest to the baniyas putting them in the debt trap. Therefore, it is suggested for timely adequate credit to the farmers by the bank.
4. There is a need for provision of strong supervision by the field staff of the bank branches with the objective of useful and productive utilisation of bank credit sanctioned to the farmers.

5. The bank should educate the people of the area about the schemes. This approach would greatly facilitate decision making by the borrowers.
6. The procedure involved in obtaining the loan should be easier and convenient for the weaker sections.
7. The sanction of a loan followed by close supervision should extend to those activities only which are found economically viable.
8. Defaulters should be given warning to repay their loans. If friendly warnings fail, there is need to give judicial punishment to the defaulters.
9. In order to prevent the diversion of credit from meeting domestic needs, the loans may be provided by the bank specially for consumption purposes.
10. Local politicians' intervention in respect of loan must be stopped and priority of sanctioning loan should extend to the lowest rung of the beneficiaries from amongst the identified weaker sections.
11. The UBKGB should improve the skills of the prospective borrowers through training, so that they can use the loans efficiently and repay them in time.
12. All the farmers should be brought under the 'National Agricultural Insurance Scheme' launched in the year 1999-2000 as the initiation of the central government aiming to provide compensation to them in case of any crop failure due to natural calamities.

Following specific steps may be taken to streamline the lending operations:

(a) The viability must be taken into account while advancing loans. Loan should be advanced only when activity for which request for loan is made is viable.

(b) The farmers must be motivated and educated to realize the fact that repayment of loan is in their interest. It will help to check willful default. This task may be performed by the bank officials and members of the farmers' club.

(c) There must be a vigorous attempt for educating the farmers that bank's loan is not a help and it is required to be repaid. Such a mental shake-up is essential so that the farmers make productive use of loans.

(d) Loan recovery camps may be arranged at panchayat level just after harvesting.

(e) In the case of cattle loan, loan should be given for two cattles so that the agricultural labourers are able to find income throughout the year.

Bibliography

1. Books

Agarwal, B. P., *Commercial Banking in India*, The Capital Publishing House, Delhi, 1983.

Arora, R. C., *Development of Agriculture and Allied Sectors*, S. Chand and Co., New Delhi, 1990.

Bhattacharya, N., *Role of Indian Rural Institutions in Economic Growth- A Critical Study*, Metropolitan Book Co. Pvt. Ltd. New Delhi, 1985.

Banerjee, P. K., *Indian Agricultural Economy : Financing Small Farmers*, Chetra Publication, New Delhi, 1977.

Kunjukunju, Benson and Mahanan, S., *Institutional Finance and Rural Development*, New Century Publications, Delhi, 2002.

Bandyopadhyay, Arun Kumar, *Economics of Agricultural Credit*, Agricole Publishers Academy, New Delhi, 1984.

Choubey, B. N., *Agricultural Banking in India*, Deep and Deep Publications, New Delhi, 1985.

Desai, Basant, *Indian Banking- Nature and Problem*, Himalaya Publishing House, Bombay, 1983.

Dhillon, D. S., *Integrated Rural Development*, Vohra Publishers and Distributors, Allahabad, 1991.

Desai, S. S. M., *Agriculture and Rural Banking in India*, Himalaya Publishing House, Mumbai, 1979.

Dar, S. U., *Impact of IRDP*, Anmol Publications, New Delhi, 1992.

Elhance, D. N. and Sharma, M. D. (Ed.), *Role of Co-operative Credit in Agricultural Development*, Orient Longman Ltd.,1968.

Gupta, S. C., *Development Banking for Rural Development*, Deep and Deep Publications, New Delhi, 1988.

Ghosal, S. N., *Agricultural Financimg in India*, Asia Publishing House, New Delhi, 1972.

Garg, Asha, *Working and Impact of IRDP*, Deep and Deep Publications, New Delhi, 1992.

Goyal, K. G., *Rural Development and banks*, Prateeksha Publications, Jaipur, 1987.

Hosamani, S. B., *Performance of RRBs- A Study*, Anmol Publications Pvt. Ltd.,New Delhi, 2002.

Jain, M. K., *Rural Banks and Rural Poor*, Printwell Publishers, Jaipur, 1989.

Joshi, P. L., *Institutional Financing in India*, Deep and Deep Publications, New Delhi,1985.

Jugale, V. B., *Co-operative Credit in Indian Agriculture*, Mittal Publications, New Delhi, 1992.

Jain, Pramod Lata, *Co-operative Credit in Rural India*, Mittal Publications, New Delhi, 1990.

Jain, S. C., *Management in Agricultural Finance*, S. Chand and Co., Delhi, 1970.

Kumar, Sunil, *Regional Rural Banks and Rural Development*, Deep and Deep Publications, New Delhi, 1990.

Kumar, Kewal, *Institutional Financing of Indian Agriculture*, Deep and Deep Publications, New Delhi, 1987.

Khatkar, R. K. , *Rural Development, IRDP in Mahendragarh District, Haryana*, Northern Book Centre, New Delhi, 1989.

Mehrotra, S. R., *Institutional Credit and Agricultural Growth*, Printwell Publishers, Jaipur, 1987.

Mathur, B. S., *Land Development Banking in India*, National Publishing House, Delhi, 1974.

Mishra, M. N., *Appraisal of Credit Facilities Provided by Banking Institutions in Rural Development*, Pragathi Prakashan, Meerut, 1987.

Mohapatra, G. P., *Rural Banks for Rural Development, Discovery of Publishing House*, New Delhi, 1997.

Mamoria, C. B., *Rural Credit and Agricultural Co-operation in India*, Kitab Mohal, Allahabad, 1983.

Mamoria, C. B., *Agricultural Problems of India*, Kitab Mohal, Allahabad, 1969 and 1977.

Naidu, K. K., *Financing of Weaker Sections by Commercial Banks*, Ashish Publishing House, 1986.

Naidu, M. C., *Financing of IRDP in India*, Discovery Publishing House, New Delhi, 1991.

Narula, R. K. and Sharma, O. P., *Agricultural and Rural Finance by Commercial Banks*, VDH Publishers, New Delhi, 1982.

Negi, Bhupal Singh, *Co-operative Credit and Regional Development- A Study of Pauri Garwal*, Deep and Deep Publications, New Delhi, 1989.

Pandhy, K. C., *Commercial Banks and Rural Development*, Asian Publication Service, New Delhi, 1980.

Pany, Kishore Raj, *Institutional Credit for Agriculture in India*, Ashish Publishing House, New Delhi, 1985.

Panda, R. K. , *Agricultural Indebtedness and Institutinal Finance*, Ashish Publishing House, New Delhi, 1985.

Pandey, Rama Nand, *Commercial Banks and Rural Development*, Deep and Deep Publications, New Delhi, 1989.

Pandey, P. C. and Jala, R. S., *Rural Development in India-Issues and Policies*, Vol. 1, Anmol Publishing Company, New Delhi,1991.

Rayudu, C. S., *Agricultural Credit and Rural Development in Drought Regions- A Study of Co-operative Banks of A. P.*, Concept Publishing Company, New Delhi, 1992.

Rayudu, C. S., *Rural Credit in India*, Mittal Publications, New Delhi, 1991.

Rao, V. G. and Malya, Paramjit, *Agricultural Finance by Commercial Banks*, Ashish Publishing House, New Delhi, 1980.

Raj, K. N., *Organizational Issues in Indian Agriculture*, Oxford University Press, New Delhi, 1990.

Ranga Reddy, A., *Agricultural Development, Rural Credit and Problems of its Recovery*, Mittal Publications, New Delhi, 1990.

Reddy, C. R., *Co-operative Long-Term Finance*, Mittal Publications, New Delhi, 1987.

Singh, J. P., *Rural Banking*, Ashish Publishing House, New Delhi, 1988.

Sinha, S. K., *Recovery of Loans From Farmers*, Deep and Deep Publications, New Delhi,1992.

Singh, B. D., *Impact of IRDP*, Anmole Publications, New Delhi, 1992.

Singh, Sukhdev, *IRDP and District Development*, Deep and Deep Publications, New Delhi, 1994.

Singh, Balwinder, *Agricultural Credit- Sources, Problems and Emerging Issues*, Deep and Deep Publications Pvt. Ltd., New Delhi, 2000.

Turan, M. S., *Institutional Finance in Rural Development*, Herman Publishing House, New Delhi, 1989.

Tyagi, Reny, *Role of Banks for Rural Development in India*, Sarup and Sons, New Delhi, 1993.

Uduman Mohideen, K.S.S., *Institutional Credit and Agricultural Development*, Mittal Publications, New Delhi,1992.

Verma, M. L., *Rural Banking in India*, Rawat Publications, Jaipur, 1988.

Veerashekharappa, *Institutional Finance for Rural Development*, Rawat Publications, Jaipur, 1997.

Wadhava, Charan, D., *Rural Banks for Rural Development- An Analysis of the Working of Regional Rural Banks in India With Two Case Studies*, The Macmillan Co. India Ltd., New Delhi, 1980.

II. Articles

Balishter, A.K., "Evaluation of Repayment Capacity of Farmers", *Indian Co-operative Review*, 21(1), pp. 90-93.

Bhattacharya, Puspitaranjana, "Problems and Prospects of Regional Rural Banks- A Case Study of Mayurakshi Grameena Bank, West Bengal", *Agricultural Bankers*, 17(1), 28-34.

Bhosale, S. R. and Dangat, S. B., "A Study into the Overdues of Co-operative Loans in Maharashtra", *Indian Journal of Agricultural Economics*, 43(3), 420

Bhavani Devi, I. and Sitaraman, S., "Analysis of Factors Influencing Repayment Capacity", *Agricultural Banker*, 8(4), 11-13.

Devasia, Leelamma, "Co-opratives and Rural Development", *Kurukshetra*, Vol. XXXV, No. 6, March 1986.

Datta, Bhabatosh, "Regional Rural Banks", Report of the Review Committee, R. B. I., *Bombay, Economic and Political Weekly*, Vol. XIII, No. 36, 1979.

Das Gupta, H. K. and Dutta, A. R., "Repaying Capacity of Small Farmers in Changing Agriculture in Dhenkanal District", *Indian Journal of Agricultural Economics*, Vol. XXVI, No. 4, October- December, 1971.

Datta, Poreshchandra, "Nationalised Banks and Agricultural

Finance", *Kurukshetra,* Vol.20,No.10, February 16, 1972.

Deb, Sharmistha and Rajeev, Meenakshi, "Banking on Baniyas for Credit", *Economic and Political Weekly,* January 27, 2007.

Gupta, S.K., "Profitability and Regional Rural Banks", *Kurukshetra,* July 1996.

Jayasheela and Birdar, R.R., " Rural Finance : A Village Study", *Kurukshetra,* Vol. 48, No.6, March 2000.

Krishnan, C., "Regional Rural Banks and Rural Development", *Yojana,* Vol.33, No.24, January 1-15, 1990.

Kamat, G.S., "Regional Rural Banks", *Khadi Gramodyog,* Vol. XXII, No.2, November 1975, pp.108-09.

Krishna Swami, O. R., "Reorganisation of Rural Banks", *Kurukshetra,* Vol. XXVI, No.2, October 16, 1977.

Mariarad, A., and Sebastian M., "Development of Small and Marginal Farmers", *Kurukshetra,* Vol. XXX(5), December, 1981.

Narayana, G. A., "Problems of Agricultural Loans", *Kurukshetra,* XXXIV(7), April, Publication Division, Government of India, New Delhi, 1987.

Prasad, K. N., "Why is Bihar Backward", *Yojana,* May, 1981.

Pandey, U. K. and Singh, I. J., "Risk and Credit Management in Changing Agriculture", *Indian Co-operative Review,* 9(1), pp. 91-103.

Ramakumar, R.and Chavan, Pallavi, "Micro-Credit and Rural Poverty-An Analysis of Empirical Evidence", *Economic and Political Weekly,* March 9, 2002.

Reddy, Gangi, "The Role of Regional Rural Banks in Credit Distribution", *Kurukshetra,* May 1988.

Raja Rao, A., "Impact of the RRBs on Income and Employment of Weaker Sections", *Kurukshetra,* Vol. XLIV, No. 10, July 1996.

Ramola, K. S. and Negi, K.S., "Regional Rural banks and Rural Development"- A Case Study, *Yojana,* 35(12), 23-25.

RBI, "Viability of RRBs, A Study", *RBI Monthly Bulletin,* XXXV, March 1981.

Hanumantha Rao, C. H., "Farm Size and Credit Policy", *Economic and Political Weekly,* Vol. V, No. 52, December 26.

Saxena, P. S., "Institutions for Rural Credit", *Kurukshetra,* Vol. 24, No. 13, April 1, 1976.

III. Theses

Betty, C. Sebastian, Regional Rural Banks and Rural Development, A Case Study With Special reference to South Malabar gramin Bank, University of Kerala, Thiruvananthapuram, M. Phil., 1992

Narasimbula, K., RRBs in Rural Development, Sri Venkiteswara University, Tirupati, Thesis (unpublished), 1988.

Shylendra, M. S., The Impact of Institutional Credit on Rural Poor With Special Reference to the Performance of RRBs in Karnataka, Bangalore University , Unpublished Thesis, 1992.

APPENDIX

Village Level Survey on Beneficiaries of UBKGB, Jalpaiguri District

Introduction

1A. District-Jalpaiguri

Village ---------

Block ----------

1B. Name of the Respondent :

Age----

Sex----

Caste SC / ST / OBC / Others

Educational Standard

Illiterate / Primary / Secondary and above

Occupational Status

Small farmers / Marginal farmers / Medium farmers / Big farmers / Agricultural labourers

1C. Family Particulars

(a) How many family members do you have?

Male---- Female------

(b) What is the number of working members in your family?

Male---- Female----

2. Resource-base/Assets Position

2A.

(i) Land holding (Area in acres)

Irrigated---

Unirrigated---

(ii) Land owned

(iii) Land cultivated

2B. House

(i) Kutcha

(ii) Pucca

3. Statement of Borrower's Economic Status

(a) Do you engage yourself in allied agricultural activities, viz., Poultry, Piggery, Dairy farming, Horticulture, Goat and Sheep-rearing, Gobar gas plants? (Tick the correct answers)

(b) If you do not occupy yourself in any allied agricultural activity, how do you utilize your leisure ? ----

(c) Do you get money order from your son/brother ? If so, how much do you get per month? Rs.----

4. Need of Agricultural Credit and Other Statements

(a) Did you Need Credit for Agricultural or Allied Agricultural Activities?

Yes/ No

(b) Did you Get Essential Credit?

Yes / No

(c) From Which Source of the Following One's Did you Get Credit for Agriculture and Allied Agricultural Activities;

Mone lender, Co-operative bank, Friends and relatives, any other source. (Tick the correct ones)

5. Need of Agricultural Credit

(a) Did you need credit for agricultural or allied agricultural activities ?

Yes/No

(b) If yes how much credit did you require to run the activity ?

(c) How much credit did you obtain from the bank ?

(d) Did you get the loans timely according to your needs ?

Yes/No

(e) How did you travel to reach the bank viz.,

Bus, Train, or Any other mode of transport? (specify)

(f) How many number of working days did you loss for this purpose ?

(g) How much did you spend to get the credit from the bank viz.,

Bus fare, Stamp charge, Stationary charge, Xerox, Searching charge, others?

(h) How often did you visit the bank premises to get the loans?

6. Problems in Getting Loan from the Bank

Did you find any difficulty in getting loans from the banks?

Yes/No

If yes, state the difficult

Delay in sanction

Delay in disbursement

Harassment by the bank staff

Lack of co-operation from the bank staff

Discriminatory behaviour of officials

Complicated loan procedure

Political intervention

Demand for bribe

Other (specify)

(Please rank the problems according to priority)

Sl. No.	Problems	Ranks
(a)		
(b)		
(c)		
(d)		
(e)		
(f)		
(g)		
(h)		
(i)		
(j)		

7. Utilisation of Credit

(a) Have you utilized the credit for the purpose for which it was sanctioned?

Yes/No

(b) If no, indicate the reasons responsible for this by specifying one or more of the following:

(i) Inadequate amount of loan,

(ii) Illiteracy and ignorance,

(iii) Poverty,

(iv) untimely credit,

(v) Spent on illness,

(vi) Lackof supervision.

(c) Have you utilized the loan for the required purpose- fully or partially?

(d) If you have utilized the loan partially for the required purpose, indicate what percentage was spent on intended purpose and what on consumption items?

(i) Percentage spent on intended purpose------

(ii) Percentage spent on consumption items-----

(e) After delivery of loan how many times did the bank staff visit the activity ?

Once/ Twice/More.

8. Repaying Capacity of the Borrowers

Have you got surplus income, deficit or neither surplus nor deficit from the loan based activity? (Please specify)

9. Refund of the Loan

(a) Have you paid the loan within the specified period? Yes/ No

(b) If yes, whether fully or partially from the loan based activity.

(c) If no, state extent of default and amount defaulted.

(d) How much amount of loan have you repaid for crop loan and business loan within the specified period?

(i) For crop loan Rs.----

(ii) For business loan Rs.---

(e) If the specified period is not yet over, do you expect to be in a position to repay the loan after completion of its time period? Yes/ No

(f) Have you repaid the loan from the additional income from the activity for which credit was taken? Yes/No

(g) If no, how did you get money for repayment?

Fresh loan/other sources. (Specify)

(h) Do you expect to be in a position to repay the loan from the income likely to be earned from the credit financed activity? Yes/No

(i) If you have not refunded the loan in time or not in a position to refund the loan in time indicate reasons responsible for it by ticking one or more of the following :

(a) Poverty,

(b) Crop diseases,

(c) Inadequate income generation,

(d) Diversion of amount for other purposes,

(e) poor monitoring,

(f) others.

10. Impact of Agricultural Credit

(a) Has your money income increased as a result of loan? Yes/No

(b) If yes, how much? (i) Before scheme Rs.---

(ii) After scheme Rs.----

(c) Did you get some additional employment? Yes/No

(d) If yes, How many months in a year?

(i) Before scheme ----

(ii) After scheme -----

(e) Improvement in the level of living of borrowers before and after availing the bank credit.

Use the following codes: '3' improved than before the scheme; '2' improved slightly before the scheme; '1' same as before the scheme.

Amenities	Quality
1. Housing	--- ----
2.Education to children	--- ----
3.Development of houses	--- ----
4.Recreational facilities	--- ----